AF566695

THE GRIFFITH FAMILY & THE FOUNDING OF GEORGETOWN

The Griffith Family & the Founding of Georgetown

Liston E. Leyendecker

University Press of Colorado

International Standard Book Number 0-87081-606-3

Published by the University Press of Colorado
5589 Arapahoe Avenue, Suite 206C
Boulder, Colorado 80303

Printed in the United States of America.

The University Press of Colorado is a cooperative publishing enterprise supported, in part, by Adams State College, Colorado State University, Fort Lewis College, Mesa State College, Metropolitan State College of Denver, University of Colorado, University of Northern Colorado, University of Southern Colorado, and Western State College of Colorado.

The paper used in this publication meets the minimum requirements of the American National Standard for Information Sciences—Permanence of Paper for Printed Library Materials. ANSI Z39.48-1992

Library of Congress Cataloging-in-Publication Data

Leyendecker, Liston E.
The Griffith family & the founding of Georgetown / Liston E. Leyendecker.
p. cm.
Includes bibliographical references (p.) and index.
ISBN 0-87081-606-3 (alk. paper)
1. Georgetown (Colo.)—History—19th century. 2. Georgetown (Colo.)—Biography. 3. Griffith family. 4. Pioneers—Colorado—Georgetown—Biography. 5. Miners—Colorado—Georgetown—Biography. 6. Colorado—Gold discoveries. 7. Frontier and pioneer life—Colorado—Georgetown. 8. Gold mines and mining—Colorado—Georgetown—History—19th century. 9. Mining camps—Colorado—History—19th century. I. Title: Griffith family and the founding of Georgetown. II. Title.

F784.G34 L485 2001
978.8'61—dc21

00-013140

Cover design by Laura Furney
Text design by Daniel Pratt

10 09 08 07 06 05 04 03 02 01 10 9 8 7 6 5 4 3 2 1

To my parents,
Joseph Patrick Leyendecker, Jr., and Madalyn Edgington Leyendecker

Contents

Illustrations

Acknowledgments

THE NICEST PART ABOUT COMPLETING A MANUSCRIPT is being able to thank the people who have helped turn an idea into a finished essay. Although this book is small, a good number of persons and organizations contributed to it.

Professor Thomas J. Noel, Department of History, University of Colorado at Denver, suggested that I write this piece. The staffs of the Stephen H. Hart Library at the Colorado Historical Society, the Western History Section at Denver Public Library, the William E. Morgan Library at Colorado State University, and the John Tomay Memorial Library in Georgetown, Colorado, all did a fine job of seeing to it that I obtained much-needed material to complete this publication.

Betty J. Budd, Mills County Genealogical Society, Myrna McManigal, Mills County Recorder, and Roberta Dashner, Deputy Mills County Recorder, all of Glenwood, Iowa, did a great deal to answer questions about the Griffith residency in Glenwood. Patricia M. Meisinger, Register of Deeds, Cass County, Nebraska, helped me with the real estate transactions of the Griffiths in Plattsmouth, Nebraska. Eric Mundell, Head of Reference Services, Indiana Historical Society, and James Smith Scott, Indiana County Historian, Milroy, Indiana, helped me trace down Jefferson and Sidney Griffith in Indiana. Elizabeth Bailey, Reference Specialist, the State Historical Society of Missouri, Columbia, Missouri, shed light on the Griffith family in Missouri. James M.

Prichard, Archivist, Kentucky Department for Libraries and Archives, Frankfort, Kentucky, helped me with the Griffith family in Kentucky.

Georgetown, Colorado, dwellers and scholars who made this a better manuscript include Brad Bailey, former Clear Creek County attorney, who furnished valuable leads in Jackson County, Colorado. Christine Bradley, Clear Creek County Archivist, provided me with numerous blurbs, maps, and census lists, which were most welcome, particularly on Jefferson and George Griffith. She also served as a sounding block for ideas that came up during the research and writing. Debbie Zarlingo, Office of the Tax Assessor for Clear Creek County, helped me find David Griffith's Georgetown home, while Jonathan Held, Curator of Properties for Historic Georgetown, Inc., garnered bits of information that contributed to the final product. Ronald J. Neely, the gentlemanly Superintendent of Historic Georgetown, Inc., rendered great service in interpreting historic photographs and by telling me where to locate them.

Professor Duane A. Smith, at Fort Lewis College, Durango, Colorado, took time from a very busy schedule to read and comment on this manuscript, while he furnished lots of encouragement. Silvia Pettem, also a Colorado historian, helped me with David Griffith's later career in the community he helped found.

Students at Colorado State University also helped out by running down tidbits in newspapers and checking courthouse records. Here, I think of Julia Langefield, Keith Kempke, Jane Maurer, and Thomas Moore, whose efforts contributed substantially to the book in front of you.

Susan Jones and Jody Griffin, both stalwarts of the Department of History at Colorado State University, did much to ease the pain of a professor when it came to getting a manuscript properly placed on a computer.

Finally, Barbara, my young bride of many years, spent much time taking pictures and producing maps.

Each of you is a part of this publication, just as much as I, although the mistakes are mine. All of you deserve a most hearty *thank you*.

THE GRIFFITH FAMILY & THE FOUNDING OF GEORGETOWN

1

Introduction

OVER THE LAST TWO DECADES I have studied nineteenth-century Georgetown, Colorado. I have turned up many interesting little details and sidelights of the years between 1859 and 1870, some of which warrant being given to the public as separate bits of memorabilia.

Such is the case with Griffith Mining District's earliest mining laws. I have looked at the old, handwritten codes several times; one thing that stood out as I read through them was that they were created by someone who was intimately acquainted with the legal and mining jargon of that period.

Historians and buffs who deal with Colorado's past know that traditional accounts of the gold rush period report that the state's early mining laws had their origins in those adopted in California a decade earlier. The "forty-niners" lifted their ordinances, in part, from earlier statutes used by the Spaniards, and later, the Mexicans. However, these endeavors were supplemented many times by English common law, which applied more directly to the unique problems encountered by separate camps. Many of the mining laws were set down by laymen who wanted swift justice unencumbered by legal technicalities and tricks. Several mining areas went so far as to bar lawyers from practicing or pleading in a lawsuit unless one of the opposing litigants was a legal practitioner. If one of the litigants was a lawyer, then the other side could use attorneys as well.

In the early days, Colorado miners faced lack of experience and knowledge of mining, simply because many were straight from the farm, or some other background. These people wanted to make their fortunes as fast as possible so they could return to their former homes, to enjoy lives of comfort they had lost in the panic of 1857.

Georgetown does not fit this pattern exactly. Its founders, members of the brood raised by Jefferson and Sidney Griffith (see Appendix 2), were land speculators and pioneer farmers who spent their lives moving first from Kentucky to Indiana, and then to Missouri. Jefferson, accompanied by his second-oldest son, George, joined the California gold rush, while the others left Missouri to settle in the Glenwood, Iowa–Plattsmouth, Nebraska area about 1853. Jefferson and George joined them after returning from California in 1857. There the family remained until 1858, when John and George, along with David, decided to participate in the Colorado gold rush in the late summer and early fall of 1858.

In Colorado, George Griffith used his mining experience as he prospected Vásquez Creek or Fork (later called South Clear Creek) and made the gold strike that led to the founding of Georgetown. Unfortunately, the small settlement that developed as a result never prospered because the area surrounding it had very little gold. The Griffiths were gold miners and their camp's early existence was directed at mining the precious metal. Although they produced some gold, they were unable to fulfill their dreams of a bonanza, even though they did their best to succeed. Ironically, the area possessed a great wealth of silver.

Those who study this camp's early period will be struck by the notion that the Griffiths attempted to set up a small family empire along South Clear Creek. Apparently, they had some money, whether because of Jefferson's land speculation activities as he moved across the lower part of the Middle West, or because he and George had enjoyed some success in California. Available records reinforce the impression that the Griffiths possessed some financing because, in 1860, they spent $1,500 to build a road from Central City to their struggling little settlement. In addition, they acquired a stamp mill, which they transported to Georgetown, at a time when money remained tight in the United States due to hard times, and apprehension over the start of the Civil War. Finally, the Griffiths operated several mines, and, during the three and a half years they worked in the vicinity, they preempted large numbers of claims including those staked and registered in nearby mining districts.

While journalists made occasional references to Georgetown, it was not until the spring of 1861 that they really began to describe and extol the camp's virtues to the outside world. Even so, while prospectors drifted in and out of the valley, the settlement boasted but forty-five permanent residents at the end of March 1861. This condition probably forced the Griffiths to run their district. George was the only one to occupy the office of recorder, while his brother, David, occupied other positions so that the family appeared destined to keep the camp's control in its hands.

The Griffiths' primary interest was to make money, so their district mining laws, which they set down and then passed, seemed to favor them. These codes were very complete, unlike many preliminary versions developed by contemporary mining districts. Griffith Mining District laws were written by attorneys since two, and possibly three, of the sons were trained in that profession. In addition, Jefferson, the father, had experience both as a pioneer farmer and as a miner. Although it is unclear who was responsible for creating the code, these men possessed some education along with enough experience to establish both agricultural and mining areas.

From 1860 to 1861, Georgetown was a sparsely populated, struggling hamlet with few, if any, amenities, which attempted to produce gold from ground that was nearly barren of that metal. It was a fine example of the basic mining camp Duane Smith describes in his *Rocky Mountain Mining Camps: The Urban Frontier*.[1] Since the Griffiths were more interested in securing their mining interests than in creating a community, they focused their efforts on mining rather than municipal codes. However, once they had formed a thorough set of mining statutes, they began addressing civic matters connected with their camp.

I have transcribed the handwritten laws of the Griffith Mining District to make them more accessible to researchers interested in such materials, while also providing background to place the codes in their historic context. These statutes go beyond the law to tell us a great deal about the early period of Colorado's "Silver Queen," providing us with a glimpse into Colorado's past.

Note

1. Duane A. Smith, *Rocky Mountain Mining Camps: The Urban Frontier* (Bloomington: University of Indiana Press, 1967), 9–10.

2

The Griffiths Arrive

On August 26, 1859, William N. Byers, editor of the *Rocky Mountain News*, reached the Georgetown mines, in what would become the state of Colorado, and furnished his subscribers with their first report of the area. Byers's party was hospitably received by dwellers in the settlement, which consisted of five men and one boy. These residents offered the recent arrivals the use of a house as long as they wanted to stay, which they accepted eagerly since they had been riding in the rain all day.

Byers informed his readers that a Kentuckian by the name of George F. Griffith had discovered a lode three or four weeks before. He proceeded to open the lead (pronounced "leed," this term is synonymous with lode), which was located high on a mountainside. He set a sluice and worked it for two days, taking out a little over $100 worth in gold, before he began to encounter difficulties—probably because the vein narrowed there. George's younger brother, David T. Griffith, had been traveling with him when he discovered the outcropping, and shortly afterward an older sibling, John S. Griffith, also joined them.[1] The brothers must have worked the lode longer than two days to accomplish the small amount of development they performed. They rolled much of the ore they took out of a dirt crevice in the Griffith Lead down the side of the mountain. Such rock paid between fifty cents and one dollar the pan, in all about $500 worth. Nevertheless,

William N. Byers, photographed here with his family at their Denver home in May 1862, made the first report of George F. Griffith's gold strike at what would become Georgetown. Courtesy Colorado Historical Society, negative #F39577.

they became discouraged as they went into cap, which they could not penetrate, and abandoned the district.[2]

Just as George made his strike, a report from the northern part of the territory surfaced telling of a very rich find in northern Larimer County, about 125 miles northwest of Denver. George dropped everything, and following the example set by no less a contemporary notable than John H. Gregory (whose strike had led to the founding of Central City and Black Hawk), he headed to the new site. George Griffith's precipitous departure indicates that his two brothers must have recovered most of the ore produced on South Clear Creek, originally known as Vásquez Creek. Later, they closed the workings and returned to the East, which explained why no Griffiths were present to greet Byers when he visited their camp.[3]

The *News* editor pointed out that two or three claims were being opened on the Griffith lead, but were not being worked properly, although they appeared very rich. Other indications of mineral wealth cropped out in the vicinity on both sides of the creek, and all looked very promising.[4]

While George pursued the possibility of a new bonanza in Larimer County, John headed for Glenwood, Iowa, to bring his wife, Elvira, and his father, Jefferson Griffith, back to Colorado. Jefferson was a "yonder sider," or a veteran of the California gold camps. John also sought supplies and more men, while David made the trek back East to secure a stamp mill.[5]

John and David were not alone in their decision to go east as summer gave way to early fall. Many miners who worked along South Clear Creek in the summer of 1859 retreated from the area as bad weather approached. By early December, cold weather finally shut down outdoor mining operations for the year. Those few hearty souls who still remained worked in drifts and tunnels, digging out ore "for the next Spring's washing."[6]

Many miners were lured by glowing reports of fabulously wealthy mineral strikes in South Park and beyond. The finds had been made during late summer 1859 and accounts soon told of very rich production. Such publicity led to a frenzy of road building from Denver to the new mining camps and an improvement of existing routes to established communities such as Mountain City.[7]

A few "fifty-niners" continued to operate west of Idaho Springs, establishing new communities during the fall of 1859 and spring of 1860. However, a good number of these miners retreated as the weather worsened and grew colder. One report in mid-October stated that nearly all the mines on South Clear Creek were abandoned for the season. On Buckeye Bar three or four sluices still operated, five were running on Union Bar, and on Spanish Bar, where a month before fifty sluices had been operating, there were only three. Frank Hall, an early Colorado historian, also observed that Spanish Bar was the camp where the Griffith brothers mined until shortly before George made his strike.[8]

In spite of the exodus of miners in autumn 1859, quite a number began retracing their steps during late December 1859 and early January 1860 to work gulch claims. Tales of such operations were

The Stanley Mill complex stands on the site of the early Clear Creek County mining camp called Spanish Bar. Photograph by Barbara B. Leyendecker.

continual, as seekers of mineral wealth either entered or returned to the area, taking advantage of the unseasonably warm weather. Soon reports stated that snow had all but disappeared from the mountain areas, and that those who had claims in operation were doing very well. Hopefuls who had not encountered such good fortune could prospect the area just as easily as though it were summer. Rumors from South Park and the Blue River diggings told that men were making between $10 and $30 per day. The *Rocky Mountain News* did not give this information much credence, and advised people not to enter the mountains beyond the Clear Creek and Gregory mines, because severe weather might reappear.[9]

Along the south, or main, fork of Clear Creek, miners began to reenter Buckeye, Union, Spanish, and other bars. There, they occupied their old cabins and claims, in a region where most of the mines were in bars and on hillsides. These mines had typically paid well. No news appeared that spring concerning the Georgetown diggings at the headwaters of Clear Creek. This was probably due to the camp's close proximity to the Snowy Range (as the miners called the Rockies), which meant the district remained filled with snow and ice. Nevertheless, as spring came, the great surge of mineral seekers continued into the mountains, until by the middle of May over five hundred men were making their way to the mines, their numbers increasing daily.[10]

The *Rocky Mountain News*, observing that the great influx into the area created a dearth of essential items, suggested that

> Somebody could make a handsome thing just now by bringing in a few wagon loads of pick and ax handles. They readily bring from a dollar to a dollar and a half each. Brooms are also out of market.[11]

AMONG THE ENTHUSIASTIC RETURNEES was John S. Griffith, heading a wagon train transporting his wife, Elvira, his father Jefferson, and a number of others. They arrived in Central City and Black Hawk Point, two communities that were rapidly developing from the original Mountain City, in mid-June. There they were met by George.[12]

The Griffiths determined to head for Georgetown immediately, but discovered they could not penetrate the virgin country between Eureka Street, on the west end of Central City, and Georgetown. They went so far as to unload their wagons and pack their equipment and supplies on the backs of animals, but to no avail. The fact remained that, despite the road-building mania to other camps, there was no route to the Griffith camp. Nevertheless, the Griffiths remained undaunted in their determination to make their way to Georgetown, in spite of the obstacles. This left them little choice but to build a roadway of their own. Therefore, they obtained the rights to build a toll road beginning at the head of Eureka Gulch, which they recorded in Central City. The road ran up Eureka Gulch, then down York Gulch and Fall River to Clear Creek. Finally, it ran westward, up Clear Creek

Central City, the "jumping off" spot for the Griffiths as they began their road to Georgetown. Courtesy Colorado Historical Society, negative #F2782.

to the site of Georgetown, a distance of some twenty-two miles.[13]

The party began building the road on June 18, 1860, and continued down York Gulch through the York, Fall River, and Iowa mining districts, which they reached after a great deal of hard labor. Iowa District residents eagerly signed a charter petition for a toll road, which George Griffith and Company entered in the district's records on July 21, 1860.[14]

The Griffiths continued their labors for several days, finally reaching the mouth of Fall River, where the Fall River Road was completed. The Fall River District members also gave their consent for the toll road to proceed through the their district. After that, the Griffiths' firm decided to build a road up Clear Creek.

Mountain City in 1860 would have been a familiar scene to the Griffiths and their contemporaries. Courtesy Colorado Historical Society.

Finally, on August 20, 1860, "their little train was pleasantly corralled upon a beautiful plateau in the Griffith District, upon which they were pleased to lay out the . . . thriving little place, Georgetown." A report from many years after the road's completion stated that the builders were headed by Cyrus Hiltibiddle, who drove the first team into the location of the future town. The road had cost $1,500 to build.[15]

The site had been laid out almost two months earlier at a meeting on June 29, 1860, when several men, including George, John, Jefferson, and William Griffith, William Renshaw, their sister Mary Griffith's husband, and other members of the party, described the location:

> Commencing at a pine tree on west side of West fork of South Clear creek marked with three notches thence East one half mile to a pine tree on East Bank of South Clear

Map showing the route of the Griffith Road. Drawn by Barbara B. Leyendecker.

Creek marked with three notches Thence North two miles to a pine tree on East Bank of South Clear Creek Thence West one half mile to a pine tree Thence South to the place of beginning Containing (640) six hundred and forty acres more or less.[16]

A photographic view of Mountain City, the early predecessor of Central City and Black Hawk. Courtesy Denver Public Library, Western History Collection, call number 11219.

Although toll roads existed throughout the territory as a necessity, miners in the area served by the Griffith Toll Road became incensed at the Griffiths for charging to use the route. Nevertheless, it was standard procedure for road builders to reimburse themselves for constructing such routes, since no public funds existed to pay for them. In other areas served by such roads, the builders also were criticized heartily by their customers. Nevertheless, the displeasure was probably an overt indication of the unpopularity of at least certain members of the Griffith family. Such indications continued to appear during their residence in the district. The Griffiths eventually disposed

This picture of the intersection of today's Main and Fourteenth Streets in Georgetown was taken about 1866–1867. The arrow points to what was probably George F. Griffith's cabin, the spot where Georgetown began. Courtesy Denver Public Library, Western History Department, call number X1439.

of the road and the subsequent owners became known as the Central City and Georgetown Wagon Road Company. An 1871 report noted that the road was traveled heavily throughout the

Detail showing what was probably George F. Griffith's cabin.

year, was maintained well at all times, and accepted all types of vehicles.[17]

During the remainder of 1860 and on into 1861, the Griffiths continued to improve their camp. David returned from the East with the stamp mill and immediately surveyed the district. The brothers also erected three cabins and made various improvements to prepare for the assembly of the stamp mill. They also took title to town lots, George claiming Lot 1 in Block 1 while David took Lot 6 in the same block. Jefferson settled on Lot 1 in Block 2, and was joined in the block by Elvira, who claimed Lots 4 and 5. John took Lot 6 in Block 2, and George also claimed Lot 1 in Block 3.[18]

Judging by the numerous claims registered in their names, the Griffiths also did a great deal of prospecting in both their

The intersection of Main and Fourteenth Streets as it appeared in July 1999. Photograph by Barbara B. Leyendecker.

own and other camps. However, George and David seemed to devote the greater part of their time to solidifying their domain through finalizing and codifying the Griffith Mining District's laws and statutes.

There was good reason for them to pursue such endeavors, because Georgetown started to grow during the spring of 1861. By the end of March, *Rocky Mountain News* reporters began visiting the camp as they extolled its virtues and scenery.

All commented on the district's beauty, located as it was on the south side of Clear Creek. Spring was starting to arrive in the tree-covered valley, as bars and bottoms turned green with grass. Georgetown, the district's headquarters, stood on a lovely site. Its proprietors and inhabitants saw to the protection of the shade trees, including cedars, junipers, and pines, along with the aspen.

Although the camp boasted only forty permanent residents, thirty-five of whom had arrived since January, they needed convenient trading facilities, and a person "with a small stock of assorted goods" would do well to set up shop there. The town boasted at least four cabins (all built by the Griffiths), and exuded a general well-being. John Griffith guided visitors through the district, since George and David were so busy revising and recodifying the district's laws and statutes. One member of the press concluded his report by thanking John and Elvira, along with the rest of the Griffith family, for their hospitality.[19]

Further research is required to determine exactly where the Griffiths' cabins stood in Georgetown. However, photographs and maps from later dates, together with property records and newspaper accounts, indicate that the center of the Griffiths' Georgetown sprang up near today's Griffith and Fourteenth Sstreets on the south, and Main and Fourteenth Streets on the north. George Griffith's cabin probably stood close to the corner of today's Fourteenth and Griffith. (At the time the Griffiths occupied the community, Fourteenth Street was Seventh Street.)[20]

The *Rocky Mountain News* reporters told of prospectors who arrived daily, many by way of the Griffiths' road, a good route between Central City and Georgetown. Seventy-five leads had been located and assays from those tested had equaled the highest expectations of their owners. Clear Creek and its branches contained enough water to supply fifty to one hundred water powers within the district. The Griffith stamp mill would start work shortly, while George Nicholls's sawmill would be operating by late April.[21]

At the end of April, the snow was disappearing and grass was growing in the valleys, after several days of good weather. This led the community to hope the good weather would continue so that miners and millmen could get to work.[22]

Prospects looked good and predictions were that enough quartz would be extracted to keep twenty mills busy. Unfortunately, the area had only three stamp mills in various stages of completion, so the district's future prosperity depended upon the arrival of more machinery. Several new leads had been discovered, including the Columbus, from which miners had removed a small amount of ore, turning it over to a Central City assayer named Howard. He analyzed the ore and pronounced it to be "as fine, if not the most valuable specimen he [had] ever [had] the pleasure of testing." Needless to say, a company was forming to prospect and develop the lead. By April 27, 1861, the number of lodes discovered had increased to eighty-two, and between 2,000 and 3,000 claims had been recorded on them.[23]

The labor required to open and work Georgetown's leads was insignificant when compared to numerous other camps. For example, the Griffiths had begun to take pay quartz from the first five feet of their tunnel, and stated that fifteen men could average ten cords from this single lode daily. At the end of April, another account's author, having spent twenty-four hours inspecting a sizable portion of the Griffith District, was "astonished" by its wealth in precious minerals, and considered it the richest of all the mining districts yet discovered.[24]

The reporter had passed a day closely examining the Griffith lode, the most extensively prospected lead in the district. The Griffiths owned 1,400 feet on the lead. It had paid handsomely from the surface where huge masses of quartz (called outcroppings) projected from the hillside. The pockets of pay dirt paid from fifty cents to one dollar per pan, while its quartz had been tested and would pay ten to fifteen cents per pound.[25]

When it came to development, one shaft had been sunk twenty-five feet on the lead and two tunnels were being dug to it, while the surface quartz, after removal, was corded into large quantities. Jefferson Griffith believed they would be millionaires in "good time."

The Griffiths also had gone to great expense to complete a 1,000-foot chute, connecting their discovery claim near the summit of Griffith Mountain to the bar beneath. They were running their quartz down to the district's first completed mill. Even the quartz removed at the surface was intermixed heavily with iron pyrites and was perhaps the wealthiest found in the Rockies up to that time. At surface level, the lead was impressive, while beneath the surface, the crevice increased greatly in width as workers descended into it. Industrious miners were hard at work exploring other leads on the Griffith.[26]

The district's first mill, built by Colonel William Davidson, a part owner in the Glove Lode, began pounding on April 24, 1861. It was a three-stamp mill, hand operated by two men, which crushed about 100 pounds of ore per day. The Griffiths continued to build their six-stamp mill (made of wood, but shod with iron), hoping to have it running by May 5. They had dug a 100-foot mill race, and enough water could be turned into it to run fifteen stamps of their own, plus other mills.[27]

At that time, there was talk of a road up Clear Creek, which, plans stated, would go through the South and North Park to reach Salt Lake City. Georgetown's future appeared auspicious, according to the journalists who visited it.[28]

To protect their interests, the authors of the Griffith Mining District's codes continued hard at work and, before they completed their task, also showed their political constituency's concern for the women of the district.

The Griffiths probably were influenced by their mother Sidney Griffith's experiences on the Indiana and Missouri frontiers, not to mention Elvira Griffith's presence in their midst, even though women were no strangers to other parts of the area. Reports as early as May 1859, made by traders arriving in Kansas City via the Santa Fe Trail, stated 220 women were on their way to the Colorado–Pike's Peak mines. Another party boasted at least one woman who was well over seventy years old and many women with their destitute families. A month later, Albert D. Richardson, a noted journalist and member of Horace Greeley's entourage to Central City, noted several women washing clothes in Gregory Gulch, and others who dressed in men's clothing.[29]

Elvira might have been the sole representative of her sex in Georgetown, but women began to put in an appearance in other, nearby mining camps, so that early in December 1860, Downieville boasted a few completed houses, and "quite a number of fine looking ladies." On March 21, 1860, Miss A. E. Carpenter had notified the ladies in Auraria and Denver that she was on the verge of opening a millinery and dressmaking establishment and would be ready to receive clients starting Saturday, March 23, 1860. Hers was the first in the area, although previously, J. H. Ming had advertised family groceries, ladies' goods, and other items. Denver prized its female residents so highly that when Apollo Hall opened on December 3, 1859, the front row was reserved for women.[30]

Other mining camps, such as Boulder and Russell's Gulch, recognized the rights of women with regard to mining claims. However, the common law Right of Dower received short shrift in Colorado's pioneer mining camps. (This law applied to the portion or interest in the real estate of a deceased husband that was given to his widow during her life.) This omission had several causes, beginning with the rugged life the miners led in the new region, which made it mostly "man's country." Women were left at home (some were deserted) in the "States" until, if all went well, they could be brought out to the new area. A number of men not only deserted their wives but changed their names as well. These complications lessened the possibility of obtaining a deed or release from a woman who lived far from her husband's final operations, and who, in all probability, was unknown to his associates. Thus, Right of Dower was discarded at the outset by custom, statute, and judicial decision.[31]

Nevertheless, the failure to use the common law's Right of Dower did not prevent Georgetown's lawmakers from inserting a foresighted enactment in their revised code, at a meeting on May 11, 1861. It stated that each of the first ten ladies to become permanent residents of the district could select one unoccupied town lot within its boundaries. Once recorded, the lot would be held by each woman as real estate.[32]

By May 1861, the Griffiths had used their expertise, gained in other frontier areas, to establish a small but functioning mining camp. They had built a good road to connect it with Central City, the largest and most prosperous mining settlement in the area. They had surveyed and set the district's boundaries, and had formulated up-to-date laws that stated how their community should function. Their stamp mill, while not actually running, was being built to process their ore. The Griffiths also sought to capitalize upon the camp's potential and scenery by guiding newspapermen through its environs, in a most hospitable manner. The penmen responded with glowing reports of Griffith Mining District. Indeed, the Griffith family's efforts seemed to have brought them to the verge of achieving the success they sought, as they advertised and developed their camp. They backed their hard work with good salesmanship.

Notes

1. David and George Griffith arrived at the settlements at the confluence of Cherry Creek and the South Platte as members of the Plattsmouth party in the fall of 1858. One report stated that John S. Griffith was a settler in Auraria during 1859. Nolie Mumey, ed., *Anselm Holcomb Barker, 1822–1895, Pioneer Builder and Early Settler of Auraria; His Diary of 1858 from Plattsmouth, Nebraska Territory, to Cherry Creek Diggings, the Present Site of Denver, Colorado* (Denver: Golden Bell Press, 1959), 61.
2. *Rocky Mountain News*, 10 September 1859, 2.
3. *Rocky Mountain News*, 13 August 1859, 2; 10 September 1859, 2; and 10 April 1861, 1. One account stated that in the spring after John and David Griffith returned to the East, they took hope when an assay of the rock from their lead showed it contained gold-bearing pyrites. When it came to George Griffith's rush to the new diggings, Charles W. Henderson, an early Colorado mining historian, wrote that little ever was heard from the workings on the Cache la Poudre. Hollister surmised they were too worthless or too hard to reach at that time. Charles W. Henderson, *Mining in Colorado: A History of Discovery, Development and Production*, United States Geological Survey Professional Paper 138 (Washington, D.C.: Government Printing Office, 1926), 7, 31. Ovando J. Hollister, *The Mines of Colorado* (Springfield, Mass.: Samuel Bowles and Company, 1867), 73.
4. *Rocky Mountain News*, 10 September 1859, 2.
5. *Rocky Mountain News*, 10 April 1861, 1. See also California Census, 1850, Broder Bund Family Archives, CD317. Census Index. U.S. Selected Counties, 1850.
6. *Rocky Mountain News*, 27 October 1859, 4; 8 December 1859, 2.
7. *Rocky Mountain News*, 13 August 1859, 2.
8. *Rocky Mountain News*, 27 October 1859, 4. See also Frank Hall, *History of the State of Colorado*, vol. 3 (Chicago: Blakely Printing Company, 1889–1893), 317.
9. *Rocky Mountain News*, 11 January 1860, 2; 18 January 1860, 2.
10. *Rocky Mountain News*, 21 March 1860, 2; 16 May 1860, 2. *The Denver Bulletin*, 9 May 1860.
11. *Rocky Mountain News*, 21 March 1860, 3.
12. Byers suggested the name Central City in late May or early June 1860. Hollister, *Mines*, 75–76. *Rocky Mountain News*, 2 May 1861, 2.

13. *Rocky Mountain News*, 2 May 1861, 2. *Private Acts, Session Laws of Colorado, 1861*, An Act to Incorporate the Central City and Georgetown Wagon Road Company, section 2, 463.
14. Iowa District, Book "A," 72–73, Clear Creek County Archives, Georgetown, Colorado.
15. *Rocky Mountain News*, 2 May 1861, 2; *Georgetown Courier*, 4 August 1900, 3.
16. Griffith Mining District, Book "A," 39, Office of the Clear Creek County Archivist, Georgetown, Colorado. The other signers were: J. D. Wood, L. W. Gibson, H. Chapeze, U. Turner, Ja. M. Taylor, M. Storms, Joshua Hobbs, John Fairchild, L. W. Wood, Jno. Russell, E. Y. Williams, G. S. Eayre, John Surber, R. M. Barker, Saml. Tush, J. Smith, J. U. St. Mathew, and Chester Colbern.

    William Griffith was supposedly a brother, but just where he fits in is unknown. One report listed a William Griffith as a member of a party that left Xenia, Clay County, Illinois, on April 4, 1860. See "Across the Plains and in Nevada City; Journal of William Cisne," *Colorado Magazine* 27, no. 1 (January 1950), 50–53. This is probably the William Griffith concerned, because Mary A. Griffith and her husband, William Renshaw, were also residents of Clay County, Illinois.
17. LeRoy R. Hafen, ed., *Colorado and Its People: A Narrative and Topical History of the Centennial State* (New York: Lewis Historical Publishing Company, Inc., 1948), 1:184–85. *Private Acts, Session Laws of Colorado, 1861*, An Act to Incorporate the Central City and Georgetown Wagon Road Company, approved November 7, 1861. T. O. Bigney and S. S. Wallihan, *The Rocky Mountain Directory and Colorado Gazetteer for 1871 . . .* (Denver: S. S. Wallihan and Company, 1870), 126.
18. Griffith District Index to Book "A."
19. *Weekly Rocky Mountain News*, 10 April 1861, 1; 12 April 1861, 2; 27 April 1861, 2; 4 May 1861, 2.
20. W. C. Willits, *Map of Brown Sherman Republican and Leavenworth Mountains*, compiled from the Official Records (Denver, Colo.: 1878). Also on the same map in a second section: W. C. Willits, *Map of Georgetown* (Denver, Colo.: 1878). Griffith District Index to Book "A," Office of the Clear Creek County Archivist, Georgetown, Colorado.
21. *Weekly Rocky Mountain News*, 10 April 1861, 1; 4 May 1861, 2.
22. *Weekly Rocky Mountain News*, 27 April 1861, 2.
23. Ibid.

24. Ibid., 27 April 1861, 2; 4 May 1861, 2.
25. *Weekly Rocky Mountain News*, 4 May 1861, 2.
26. Ibid.
27. *Weekly Rocky Mountain News*, 4 May 1861, 2; (Georgetown) *Mining Review*, January 1873, 3–5.
28. *Weekly Rocky Mountain News*, 4 May 1861, 2.
29. George M. Willing, "Diary of a Journey to the Pike's Peak Gold Mines in 1859," ed. Ralph P. Bieber, *Mississippi Valley Historical Review* 14, no. 3 (December 1927), 362–64; Albert D. Richardson, *Beyond the Mississippi: From the Great River to the Great Ocean . . . 1857–1867* (Hartford, Conn.: American Publishing Company, 1867), 181, 200.
30. *Weekly Rocky Mountain News*, 10 November 1859, 3; 22 December 1860, 4; 21 March 1860, 3. William S. Greever, *The Bonanza West* (Norman: University of Oklahoma Press, 1963), 170.
31. Henry A. Dubbs, "The Unfolding of Law in the Mountain Region," *The Colorado Magazine* 3, no. 4 (October 1926), 128–29.
32. "Real estate" in miners' parlance meant that a piece of claimed ground was not forfeited by absence. Samuel Cushman, *The Mines of Clear Creek County, Colorado* (Denver: Times Steam Printing House, 1876), 6.

3

The Early Mining Laws of Griffith District

THE GRIFFITHS SUPERVISED THE BUILDING of their toll road between Central City and Georgetown, and they were present at the signings of rights-of-way and permits from the various mining districts through which the road passed. However, once that was completed, their chief interest appeared to lie in organizing their mining camp and establishing laws by which to govern it. Here, they differed little from their contemporaries, except for having a more proprietary interest in the camp that was springing up after George's discovery.

Legal codes were not new to those who took part in the rush to the western Kansas gold fields. There were laws on the overland trails, because the travelers realized that once they crossed the Missouri River they had left civilization and its legal restraints behind. The argonauts established individual codes for each wagon train.

Miners who trekked to what would become the state of Colorado mingled with mining veterans, who had gained experience in Michigan, Georgia, and California. The mining elite, the Cornish, seldom entered a new mineral area until it proved itself. Certainly the "yonder siders" brought not only mining procedural skills, but mining codes as well, when they came to Colorado. Thus, early Colorado miners and prospectors were equipped through prior experience to begin their ventures in the new territory. At the outset, veterans of California typically made the first large strikes.[1]

The earliest gold seekers, who entered this area during 1859 to 1860, were trespassers. The area belonged to local Indian tribes, because the federal government had signed three treaties with them within the previous decade. The first was concluded with the Ute tribe in 1849, promising the Ute they could remain within their traditional borders. The United States received permission to found Indian agencies and military posts in the area.

The government in Washington, D.C., executed two treaties with the Plains Indians, both of which attempted to guarantee travelers safe passage through Indian lands on the Oregon and Santa Fe Trails. The Treaty of Fort Laramie (1851) assured the Cheyenne and Arapaho that they possessed the land that lay between the Arkansas and North Platte Rivers. The Treaty of Fort Atkinson (1853) conceded that the Comanche and the Kiowa owned the land south of the Arkansas River.

While these treaties were usually upheld in the early 1850s, conflict between Native Americans and immigrants led the army to mount a campaign against the Cheyenne in the summer of 1857. The soldiers and Indians clashed in Kansas, and the Cheyenne were badly beaten, which led to a period of relative peace during the first gold strikes.

Even though the whites settled on lands owned by the Indians, it was impossible to acquire title to them. Therefore, to protect their interests after making a paying strike, the early miners organized mining districts, establishing rules by which they could claim a share of the locale's riches. Because there was no formal authority, the miners in each district created a self-governing settlement, with authority over anyone who lived within its borders. These systems worked; these governments remained in force until the territorial legislature, and then Congress, recognized them.[2]

Once a camp had been organized, its residents followed a fairly set routine. Professor Thomas Maitland Marshall highlighted the progression by writing

> [T]he first codes to be adopted were simple, and as conditions changed, the miners found it necessary to revise, amend, and recodify the laws. The later enactments were more complex and more technical than the earlier laws, and new offices with clearly defined functions were created.

Professor Percy S. Fritz elaborated and simplified Marshall's theme by pointing out that every organized district installed four essential items: (1) the name of the district, (2) the boundaries of the district, (3) officers to execute its laws, and (4) laws regulating the size and ownership of mining claims.[3]

Colorado miners were among the earliest in the West to value simplified legal procedures, where substantial justice would be practiced in each case and legal technicalities or tricks would not be permitted to defeat its ends. Because of these priorities, several districts also passed regulations that prevented lawyers from pleading in that district's courts unless they were parties to the lawsuit; if they were parties to the suit, the opposing parties also could use attorneys. If attorneys pleaded a case other than their own, despite the ruling, they could be fined or given from ten to twenty-five lashes on the bare back. Nevertheless, in time, lawyers became a definite presence in Colorado.[4]

California districts furnished their officers with Spanish titles, but in Colorado, the officials received American titles. In some districts, such as Boulder, women were entitled to hold claims as well as men. Griffith District followed this practice. Like several other mining districts, the Griffith enclave retained the practice of giving an extra claim to the discoverer of a lode; this was a legacy of the Spanish and Mexican codes.[5]

The Griffiths certainly possessed the necessary qualifications to found a mining community. Jefferson Griffith was experienced in moving into pioneer areas both in Indiana and Missouri, and had acquired mining experience in California. George had gone to California with his father, and he too was an experienced miner, who also may have been a lawyer. John, George's older brother, was an attorney who had practiced in such newly established areas as Plattsmouth, Nebraska, and Glenwood, Iowa. He had spent time in other Colorado settlements, and certainly would have been able to call upon his legal expertise in setting up basic laws for the Griffith District. David, a surveyor, had been admitted to the bar in Central City and had practiced law in that community. Thus, Jefferson Griffith and his sons possessed the necessary experience and training to place their district on a firm legal footing. The record does not reveal how much William Griffith and William

Renshaw contributed to the founding of the camp, as they apparently chose to remain in the background. As early as June 25, 1860, several days before they laid out the site for Georgetown, the Griffiths began to establish their district's first set of mining laws.[6]

Griffith District's First Laws

The record states that a group of miners were called together to formalize a code of laws to govern Griffith Mining District. The assemblage consisted of twenty-three people, including the Griffiths and their sister Mary's husband, William Renshaw. As we have seen, George's strike did not attract hordes of interested prospectors to the site.

As their first order of business, they elected George F. Griffith recorder of the district to serve until June 25, 1861. E. Y. Williams was chosen judge of the district's Miners' Court, to serve for one year; the assemblage also selected R. M. Barker as sheriff of the district, also to serve for one year.

Following their selection of officers, the group outlined the district's boundaries, beginning:

> At a high point of rock on the West side of Clear Creek some half mile above the junction of said streams, extending one mile and a half on each side of said stream in breadth, and running up Clear Creek to the junction of the stream a short distance above the house of George F. Griffiths & Company. Thence up said streams three miles, and extending in breadth one mile, and a half from the banks of each stream.[7]

Next, they resolved that all mill, lode, and gulch claims taken during 1859, along with building lots, which were represented by an authorized person on June 15, 1860, could be held by the original claimants, but any claim taken but unrepresented on June 15, 1860, was forfeited and could be claimed by others.

Any laws passed prior to the meeting of June 25, 1860, were declared null and void. This action cancelled any rules established by those who had occupied the Griffiths' camp during their absence.

All gulch claims could extend 100 feet up the gulch or stream, and the entire width on each side. No mining claim of any kind,

Several generations of Georgetown jurors listened to lawyers' pleadings while seated in these rocking chairs. Photograph by Barbara B. Leyendecker.

including a gulch claim, could be taken if it interfered with a quartz mill site, mill yard, or any kind of building previously claimed, unless the owner gave his assent.

All lode claims were to be no more than 100 feet long and extend no farther than 50 feet on each side of the lode. (The dimensions were changed to 100 feet in length and 25 feet on each side of the lode in September 1860.)

The discoverer of a lode was entitled to a discovery claim and one additional claim, both of which had to be filed for record in the recorder's office within five days.

No one could stake a claim on any lode still being prospected by the discoverer. Any person committing such an act would be fined no less than $50 nor more than $500. No person was to take up or claim more than 100 feet on any lode except in the name of the company he might represent. Such person could take possession of up to one claim for each member of a firm represented.

Anyone who took up water claims after June 25, 1860, would be entitled to no more than 300 feet on a single stream, whether by first claim or by preemption, but a representative of a firm could claim 300 feet for each member of the company in different streams in the district.

All mining and mill claims, along with claims of any nature and building lots assigned by preemption, had to be filed in the recorder's office within five days of preemption.

The purchase or sale of any claim related to mining had to be made in writing and the transfer or bill of sale filed in the recorder's office within ten days of the transaction's consummation.

The recorder's fee for recording claims, bills of sale, and transfers for individuals would be $1. When a company was involved in one bill of sale or transfer of a claim, the recorder's fee would be fifty cents for each individual connected with the organization.

All lawsuits brought before the judge of the Miners' Court entitled the magistrate to a $2 fee for each case. All such charges were to be paid in advance by the plaintiffs. If the parties to a particular suit were not satisfied with the judge's decision, they could appeal to a jury of six district citizens, whose decision would be final.

The judge also was entitled to a fee of $1 for each summons or subpoena he might issue from his office. The sheriff was entitled to a fee of $1 for each summons or subpoena, and $1.50 for each juror.

Each member of a jury, when summoned, was entitled to $1. In all cases the plaintiff paid in advance, but after the final decision was rendered, the defeated party or parties paid. All cases could be tried in five days after a summons was issued, and the judge could hold his court on any Monday.

Once the final judgment was rendered, the sheriff could make his levy, advertise the property in three public places in the district, and offer the property for sale at public auction, ten days after the levy had been made to the highest and best bidder.

The meeting of June 25, 1860, also dealt with laws regarding ranching claims.

Any individual could claim 160 acres of land for ranching purposes (the Griffiths took up several ranching claims); an individual also could claim 160 acres of land for each member of a company he represented, and stake the land in the names of those who claimed the property. Such parcels had to be filed with the district recorder within five days of being taken or claimed.[8]

Anyone who worked a lode by means of a tunnel was entitled to 200 feet on each side of the tunnel's passage. However, the tunnel's side lodes could not interfere with any vested rights.

Any member of a company could represent the firm's claims, and such claims must be worked within three months of the time the claims had been filed for record; however, any company that operated one claim would keep, without working, all other claims it held in the district.

All water claims or mill sites would be held unimproved from the time they were taken and filed for record.

Revisons and Updates to the Laws

In a meeting held on January 12, 1861, the Griffith District miners discussed the matter of suffrage in the district. A legal voter in Griffith District was defined as any person who held a duly recorded claim in the district. All votes for district officers would be by ballot, and the district president and recorder would serve as the election's Board of Canvassers.

Any officer of the district who left its limits for more than sixty days would forfeit the office, which would be declared vacant. Any officer about to leave the district for a length of time should appoint a deputy to act in his absence. If an office was vacated before the end of a term, new officers would be elected in a specially called meeting. Since there were vacancies in two district offices, the group held an election whereby James Burrell was elected president and Cyrus Hiltibiddle sheriff.

During the meeting, a committee was formed to measure and number the water or mill privileges in Griffith District.

Members of the gathering also decided that the Griffith District sheriff should enforce the resolution that no one should take from Griffith District to any other district any wood square, building timber, or logs of any kind. Anyone who did so would be fined $50 for the first offense, and $100 for every succeeding offense. Half of the fine would go to the informer, and one half to benefit the district.

Another meeting was held on January 26, 1861, in which the committee appointed to count and measure the water or mill claims of Griffith District reported they had found: seventy-one claims, sixty-nine of which were full claims of 300 feet each, and two fractional claims, one containing 241 feet, the other 140 feet. A meeting held on March 2, 1861, allowed the miners to deal with a few important issues. They decided to create a committee to confer with a similar group from Union District to define and establish territorial boundaries between the two districts. A second committee was formed to codify and revise the Griffith District's laws.

The group also resolved that all timber designated as house logs must be used within ten days of felling unless it could be shown that an unavoidable accident had prevented use. All saw logs had to be hauled to their intended mill site within thirty days of their felling, having been marked and trimmed at the time they were cut down. Finally, all timber lying on the ground at the time of the meeting would be forfeited within thirty days. Such timber would become the common property of the district.

James Burrell, first president of Griffith Mining District. (Picture appears in History of Clear Creek and Boulder Valleys, Colorado, *1880, p. 45.)*

The Griffiths had good reason to use care in conserving their district's timber because wood was a very valuable commodity that many pioneers wasted. It was used in building homes, mills, and mining structures along with bridges and flumes. It also served a host of other uses including mine supports and fuel. The Griffiths realized that settlers in their district would need wood for shelter and business. They knew full well from their experiences in other frontier mining camps that once wood was gone residents of a district had to go far afield to locate it, and then at a premium price. Therefore, as experienced frontier land developers, they knew the value of guarding the district's timber stands. The photograph on page 13 shows how the newly formed community of Central City had lost no time in denuding its surrounding hills of available timber, a wastefulness that would soon haunt that camp.

On March 9, 1861, a meeting was held in which the boundary committee reported that a permanent boundary had been established between the Griffith and Union Districts. The group also resolved to copy the original laws of Griffith Mining District into a book for that purpose, except for laws repealed by the revised laws adopted March 9, 1861. The revised laws would also be copied into the book. The recorder would undertake this task, with a reasonable compensation to be paid from unappropriated funds in the treasury.

The results of an election held March 16, 1861, to elect district officers for the next year were James Burrell as president and judge of the Miners' Court;[9] George Griffith as recorder; P. McLain as sheriff; and David Griffith as surveyor.

Interestingly enough, nepotism began to enter the scene as George Marshall and John Griffith were the election judges, while George and David Griffith served as its clerks.

The Revised Laws

The copied and codified laws appeared in a book containing resolutions from the meetings dating from September 22, 1860. None of the laws passed on June 25, 1860, survived to be entered into this new book. The ledger began by listing the boundaries of Griffith District, before identifying the district officers, which

The original ledgers containing the early laws of Griffith Mining District. Photograph by Barbara B. Leyendecker.

were president, judge of the Miners' Court (held by the same man), sheriff, surveyor, and recorder, who also would serve as treasurer and secretary for the district. Several sections then described the methods of election and removal from office.

Next, a series of chapters described the various duties of the different officers. This was followed by a chapter describing fees the officers could charge. Chapter 9, which followed, covered the laws of the Miners' Court, many of which dealt with procedures to be observed during trials. Chapters 10 through 15 covered notices, publication, equity, exemption, redemption, and citizenship. The citizenship resolution stated that any male eighteen years of age who had lived in the district ten days immediately preceding the election was entitled to vote.

Chapter 16 dealt with criminal laws, and chapter 17 defined claims. Following sections dealt with laws covering claims and tunnel law. The final chapters concerned lot regulation, incorporations, election laws, and file laws. Other meetings after the revised code appeared, and concerned amendments to the laws, standing timber on town lots, mortgage and lien laws, and legal claim holders who were forced by circumstance to leave the district to return to the States.

Samuel Cushman, an early-day mining historian of both Gilpin and Clear Creek Counties, noted that the miners' proceedings would prove the ability of American citizens to govern themselves under any circumstances. Cushman believed that the laws set down in Griffith Mining District, after revision and codification in 1861, were probably the most complete set of laws adopted in any district in the unorganized territory.[10] Perhaps, then, the major legacy the Griffiths left behind was their very complete set of mining laws for Griffith District.

Notes

1. John Rowe, *The Hard Rock Men: Cornish Immigrants and the North American Frontier* (Liverpool, U.K.: Barnes and Noble, 1974), 190. John Phillip Reid, "Punishing the Elephant: Malfeasance and Organized Criminality on the Overland Trail," *Montana, The Magazine of Western History* 47, no. 1 (spring 1997), 4. Frank Fossett, *Colorado: Its Gold and Silver Mines, Farms and Ranges, and Health and Pleasure Resorts* (New York: C. G. Crawford, 1880), 122.
2. Carl Ubbelohde, Maxine Benson, and Duane Smith, *A Colorado History*, 7th ed. (Boulder, Colo.: Pruett Publishing Company, 1995), 189. LeRoy R. Hafen, ed., *Colorado and Its People: A Narrative and Topical History of the Centennial State*, vol. 1 (New York: Lewis Historical Publishing Company, Inc., 1948), 134, 199. J. Donald Hughes, *American Indians in Colorado* (Boulder, Colo.: Pruett Publishing Company, 1977), 54–56. Percy Stanley Fritz, *Colorado: The Centennial State* (New York: Prentice Hall, Inc., 1940), 121–22.
3. Thomas Maitland Marshall, "The Miners' Laws of Colorado," *American Historical Review* 25 (April 1920), 428. Fritz, *Colorado*, 123.
4. Gordon Morris Bakken, *The Development of Law on the Rocky Mountain Frontier: Civil Law and Society, 1850–1912* (Westport, Conn.:

Greenwood Press [Contributions in Legal Studies, no. 27], 1983), 25. Marshall, "Miners' Laws," 438. See also Duane A. Smith, *Rocky Mountain Mining Camps* (Bloomington: Indiana University Press, 1967), 165–66.

5. James Grafton Rogers, "The Mining District Governments of the West: Their Interest and Literature," *Law Library Journal* 28 (July 1935), 252. Percy Stanley Fritz, "The Constitutions and Laws of Early Mining Districts—In Boulder County, Colorado," *University of Colorado Studies* 21, no. 2 (March 1934), 134, fn. 27. Fritz, *Colorado*, 140–41. The most up-to-date summary of western mining law's legacy from the Spanish and Mexican mining codes appears in Ray August, "Gringos vs. Mineros: The Hispanic Origins of Western Mining Law," *Western Legal History: The Journal of the Ninth Judicial Circuit Historical Society* (summer/fall 1996), 147–75.
6. David S. Digerness, *The Mineral Belt*, vol. III, *Georgetown–Mining–Colorado Central Railroad* (Silverton, Colo.: Sundance Publications, Limited, 1982), 47, 161. See also Frank Hall, *History of the State of Colorado*, vol. 3 (Chicago: Blakely Printing Company, 1889–1893), 317.
7. Book "A," p. 1, Office of the Clear Creek County Archivist, Georgetown, Colorado.
8. See Book "D," p. 48, Office of the Clear Creek County Archivist, Georgetown, Colorado, for a list of the ranching claims owned by the Griffiths.
9. James Burrell was born in Bucksport, Maine, on March 29, 1815. He was apprenticed to a "house and ship joiner" and attended common schools in Maine. Upon completion of his apprenticeship, he taught school for two years before engaging in several businesses on the East Coast. He moved his family to Grinnell, Iowa, in 1858, and then to Colorado in 1860. There, he worked in Gilpin County and helped build and operate a stamp mill for the Central City firm of Hawk and Nuckolls in Chase Gulch. Later, this mill became known as the Casey Mill.

   Burrell transferred his operations to Georgetown and in the winter of 1860–1861, he helped the Griffiths complete the organization of the Griffith Mining District. He also superintended construction of Georgetown's first stamp mill. Aaron Frost, "History of Clear Creek County," in *History of Clear Creek and Boulder Valleys, Colorado* (1880; reprint ed., Evansville, Ind.: Unigraphic, Inc., 1971), 435–36.
10. Samuel Cushman, *The Mines of Clear Creek County, Colorado* (Denver: Times Steam Printing House, 1876), 6.

4

Epilogue

THE SPRING OF 1861 climaxed the Griffith family's influence in the mining district. Events moved swiftly, so that by the end of the year, the family's position had undergone substantial changes. These began when Jefferson Griffith died very suddenly on April 30, 1861, and was buried in Mill City (today's Dumont). Mr. Griffith was a very popular man who seemed a steadying influence on his sons, which kept down the strife caused by their sibling rivalries.[1]

After their father's death, the brothers began to quarrel, leading John and William to concentrate their efforts in the area that shortly would become Elizabethtown. George and David remained in the community they had founded. Family members began to leave the district as early as July 1861, when Elvira and John sold their interests to David and George prior to moving back to Glenwood, Iowa.[2] John died either in St. Louis, or in St. Joseph, Missouri in February 1881. I was unable to locate any information on Elvira after the move back to Glenwood.[3]

William Renshaw and William Griffith also sold their interests to George and David before they moved from the area. Their trail remains unclear, although William Renshaw probably returned to Clay County, Illinois. William Griffith may have joined the Colorado Volunteers and afterward spent the rest of his life in Denver working as an expressman.[4]

Although Alfred E. Mathews titled his pencil sketch "Elizabethtown," it is Georgetown about 1866 as seen from the mouth of the Griffith Tunnel. Courtesy Colorado Historical Society, negative #F8, 345)

After giving George his power of attorney, David left Georgetown as a member of the Third Colorado Volunteers. He was mustered out near Leavenworth, Kansas, where he married Lovina Smith, a widow with a daughter named Mary. There, he practiced law, and became a lay preacher for the Methodist church. David and his family returned to Georgetown in 1867, where he assumed the management of the Wilson and Cass properties. He purchased a house next to the Methodist church, and practiced law along with preaching. Later, he opened a law office in Leadville. David Griffith died in Georgetown on March 11, 1882. Several years later, his widow married Charles Fish, a Georgetown lawyer and banker, and her daughter Mary married Charles H. Morris, a mining engineer.[5]

George was the last Griffith to leave the mining district, but not before he did all in his power to make it pay. He became a

The Wilson and Cass Gold Mining Company's mill, which David T. Griffith managed after his return to Georgetown in 1867. Courtesy Denver Public Library, Western History Collection, call number F40300-8.

partner of Stephen Friel Nuckolls, one of the leading business lights of the territory.

Stephen Nuckolls was born in Grayson County, Virginia, on August 16, 1825. After completing preparatory studies, he moved to Linden, Missouri, in 1846. He was there until 1853, earning his living as a merchant. By 1854, Nuckolls had gone to Nebraska Territory, where he established a bank, helped found Nebraska City, and served in several political offices. In 1859, Nuckolls moved to Central City to engage in business and banking. In 1860, his firm, Nuckolls and Hawk, was reputedly the most successful in Central City. Nuckolls also became interested in mining and did some work near Empire before associating with George Griffith in 1863.[6]

Stephen F. Nuckolls, the Central City entrepreneur who not only bought most of the Griffith holdings, but who also formed a partnership with George F. Griffith in an attempt to bolster Georgetown's lagging fortunes. Courtesy American Heritage Center, University of Wyoming.

David T. Griffith, Lovina, his wife, and their daughter, Mary, about the time they moved to Georgetown. Courtesy Colorado Historical Society, negative #F4062.

GRIFFITH MINING DISTRICT,

KANSAS TERRITORY.

Lode Burrell

Malony W.H.

Book C

Page 67

Fees 3.00 paid

HERALD PRINT, DENVER.

Be it Known that W.H. Malony has filed and Recorded Claim No 6 W.E. from Discovery Claim on the Burrell Lode

Given under my hand this 5th day of July A.D. 1861.

Geo. F. Griffith Recorder.

Recorder's receipt signed by George F. Griffith. Courtesy Clear Creek County Archives.

Together, Griffith and Nuckolls attempted, albeit unsuccessfully, to revive the failing camp. Nuckolls renovated the Griffith stamp mill before journeying to New York City in 1863, where he organized the What Cheer Company, Wilson and Cass Company, Washington Mining Association, and the Georgetown Mining Company.[7] These firms were part of the great speculation boom between 1863 and 1864 that led to a depression in Colorado until 1868. Nuckolls and his wife, Lucinda, bought the Griffith interests and built a large log mill in the lower end of town, which blew down on Thanksgiving Day, 1869. Nuckolls retained interests in Georgetown until moving to Cheyenne (Dakota Territory) in 1867 to open a store and enter that territory's politics.[8]

Stephen Nuckolls's younger brother, Columbus or "Lum," joined his brother in the Georgetown ventures. Lum Nuckolls also served as Gilpin County treasurer for nearly a decade during the 1860s. The Nuckolls family were old acquaintances of the

Griffiths. Lum and his wife Leah had resided in Glenwood, Iowa, during the 1850s and had boarded David Griffith in 1856.

After George sold all the Griffith interests to the Nuckolls, Stephen formed mining parcels and companies, which he sold in New York during the speculation boom of 1863–1864. In 1865, George visited in Durango, Mexico, to examine a silver mine for Stephen Nuckolls, Hiram P. Bennet, and others. Shortly after, George moved to Mexico where he became a mine superintendent. He died in Austin, Texas, on August 23, 1880.[9]

Georgetown slumbered with little or no activity until a strike in September 1864 alerted miners that silver existed in the camp's vicinity. It took two years to get ore production under way, but by 1867, the old gold camp enjoyed a rebirth and was flourishing by the end of the decade. Georgetown became Colorado's first major silver center.

Notes

1. *Daily Rocky Mountain News*, 8 May 1861, 2, col. 4. Benjamin Draper, "Feudin' and Fightin': 1860," *Rocky Mountain News*, 6 June 1948, A-12.
2. Records of transactions made by John and Elvira Griffith when they sold their interests and returned to Glenwood, Iowa, can be found in the Griffith District Records, Book "E" Deeds, 38, 40, 41, 43, and 44. These transactions took place on July 16, 1861. John and Elvira sold their properties to George and David Griffith for about $14,000. Their names continued to appear in property books for several more years as they disposed of individual pieces of property.
3. For John's date of death see the *Georgetown Courier*, 16 March 1882, 3, col. 4.
4. David S. Digerness, *The Mineral Belt*, vol. III, *Georgetown-Mining-Colorado Central Railroad* (Silverton, Colo.: Sundance Publications, 1982) . A William R. Griffith appeared as a trustee of the Griffith District Gold Company in New York during April 1864. The firm had developed the Griffith, Coris Annie, Democrat, and Crawford lodes in the Griffith Mining District. Presumably William R. Griffith was the William Griffith who worked in the district. Griffith District Gold Company "Prospectus." Western History Department, Denver Public Library, Mi-Co Mines. Clear Creek County, Colo., Griffith District.

5. For David Griffith's activities, see Book "C," 625–626 and 584, (Office of the Clear Creek County Archivist, Georgetown, Colorado). See also, Book "T," 263–264, where he is listed as a married man. Following his return to Georgetown in 1867, newspaper articles appearing between 1867 and 1882 often featured his activities, although he was gone much of the time. A summary of much of his work appears in his obituary in the *Georgetown Courier*, 16 March 1882, 3, col. 2. Record of David Griffith's work with the Wilson and Cass Gold Mining Company may be found in "Wilson and Cass Gold Mining Company, Cash Book, 1864–1870." This document is in the possession of Silvia Pettem of Longmont, Colorado.
6. *Biographical Directory of the American Congress, 1774–1971* (Washington, D.C.: Government Printing Office, 1971, 1479). *Georgetown (Colorado) Courier*, 10 February 1912, 5. Frank Fossett, *Colorado: Historical, Descriptive and Statistical Work on the Rocky Mountain Gold and Silver Mining Region* (Denver: Daily Tribune Steam Printing House, 1876).
7. *Georgetown Courier*, 27 March 1884, 3.
8. Most of the Griffiths sold George and David their interests, which George and David then sold to Stephen F. and Lucinda Nuckolls. For the Nuckolls's purchases of the Griffith interests see Book "C," 487–488; Book "D," 43–47, 226–27, 378–81, and 396; Book "P," 150–51. All volumes are held in the office of the Clear Creek County Archivist, Georgetown, Colorado.
9. *Daily Mining Journal* (Black Hawk, Colo.), 12 June 1865, 3, cols. 1, 2. See also, George Griffith's obituary in *Colorado Miner*, 28 February 1880, 3, col. 6.

Appendix 1

Early Mining Laws of Griffith Mining District, 1859-1861

Transcribed by Liston E. Leyendecker
August 1997

Prefatory Note

The two original manuscripts of Griffith Mining District laws and minutes of meetings were the sources for these transcriptions. George F. Griffith and then David T. Griffith recorded the laws and minutes. I have attempted to make my transcription as close to the original manuscripts as possible, given mistakes and omissions that *will* occur no matter how much care a transcriber may devote to a project of this nature. A few words were illegible, and I've indicated this with brackets. There were remarkably few illegible words in the original documents.

One may only marvel at the dedication and perseverance of the Griffiths as they labored over these pieces, recording them in the copy ledger books of the era, by candlelight, on homemade desks, using steel dip pens, and quite possibly home-manufactured ink. The recorders unconsciously left a record of their fatigue in penmanship that became more of a scrawl and words omitted from the text. Nevertheless, the Griffiths stuck to their task, which left future generations a priceless record of their lives in very early Georgetown.

The brothers entered the laws in two slim commercially produced ledger books of the period. The first, "Book A of Griffith Mining District" (the complete title is on the first page inside the cover) contains Griffith District's first mining laws, beginning on

June 25, 1860, and ending on March 26, 1861. These appear on pages 1–13 and 128–31 of Book A. The remaining pages, 16–123 and 130 to the end of the book, are dedicated to very early claim registrations that I did not include in my transcription.

The second ledger runs from March 26, 1861, to July 17, 1861, and contains the recopied and recodified laws on pages 1–39. This second book is entitled "Laws of G D," which was written in pencil inside the front cover, probably at a later date.

Both these volumes are held in the office of the Clear Creek County Archivist, Georgetown, Colorado.[1]

Note: The spelling, punctuation, and capitalization in the original documents have not been changed.

Griffiths District June the 25th 1860

The Miners of this Destrict having meet on this day, and date above mentioned according to previous notice given and formed The following code of Laws of which this destrict shall be hereafter governed.

1st Resolved,

That George F. Griffith is hereby elected Recorder of this Destrict to serve as Recorder from this date until June the 25th 1861.

2d Resolved,

That E. Y. Williams is hereby elected Judge of the Miners Court of the Said Destrict to have and to hold Said Office from this above mentioned date until June the 25th 1861.

3rd Resolved,

That R. M. Barker is hereby elected Sheriff of this Destrict to have and to hold Said Office from this date until June 25th 1861.

4th Resolved,

That Said Griffiths Destrict Shall be bounded as follows, Commencing at a high point of Rock on the West Side of Clear Creek Some half mile above the Junction of Said Streams, extending one mile, and a half on each Side of Said Stream in breadth, and running up Clear Creek to the Junction of the Stream a short distance above the House of George F. Griffiths & Company. Thence up Said Streams three miles and extending in breadth one mile, and a half from the Banks of Each Stream.

5th Resolved,

All claims taken and claimed for Mill purposes, Lode Claims, Gulch Claims, Building Lots taken, and claimed in the year of Eighteen hundred and fifty-nine and represented by the Party or Partys or their agent or agents on the fifteenth day of June last Shall be and are hereby held by Said Party or Parties, So having taken Them, But all claims of any character whatever taken, and claimed heretofore, and unrepresented on the fifteenth day of June 1860 are hereby forfeited and liable to be taken up by Other Parties.

6th Resolved,

All Laws passed heretofore by any previous Meeting Shall be and are hereby Repealed, and shall be hereafter Null and Void.

7th Resolved,

All Gulch Claims may extend one hundred feet up the Gulch or Stream, and the entire width on each Side of Said Gulch or Stream.

8th Resolved,

No Gulch Claim or Claim of any kind shall be taken for Mining purposes where It interferes with a Quartz Mill Sight previously taken by another Party or Parties or Mill house or Mill yard, of the same, or a building of any kind unless it be by the Written Consent of the proper Owner or Owners of the Same,

9th Resolved,

All Lode Claims Shall be no more that One hundred feet in length and extending fifty feet on each side of the Lode.

10th Resolved,

The Discoverer of any Lode shall be entitled to the Discovery Claim and One Claim in addition to the Discovery Claim on Said Lode Which He Shall file for Record in the Office of the Recorder in five days after completeing such Discovery, and prospecting.

11th Resolved,

No Person or Persons Shall be permitted to set stakes upon or take a Claim on any Lode while the Discoverer is prospecting the Same and He shall have taken one Claim in addition to the One discovered, which He Shall do in five days after making such discovery, and completing His prospecting the Same. Any one so offending Shall be fined not less than fifty dollars and no more than five hundred dollars.

12th Resolved,

No Person Shall take up, and claim more than one hundred feet on any one lode except in the name of the Company He may represent. He or they may take up One Claim for each Member of the Company He or They may Represent.

13th Resolved,

All Persons taking up Watter Claims hereafter Shall not be entitled to more than Three Hundred feet on Said Stream of Preemption or any one Stream but Any Person representing a company may take up, and claim three hundred feet for each member of said company, in the different streams in Said District.

14th Resolved,

All Claims for Mill purposes Mining purposes, Claims of any character building lots acquired by preemption must be filed for record in the Office of the Recorder in five days after such preemption has been taken and such premtion must be marked where Taken.

15th Resolved,

All claims of any character whatever acquired by purchace or Sales of any kind relating to mining must be made in writing, and the Transfer or Bill of Sale must be filed for Record in the Office of the Recorder in Ten Days after such Transfer or Sale is Made.

16th Resolved,

All Claims taken by one Individual in Recording Transfers, Bills of Sale the fee of the Recorder Shall be one dollar but where a company is embraced in one Transfer or Bill of Sale or Claim then his fee shall be fifty cents for each individual embraced in said Company.

17th Resolved,

All cases of Litigation comming before the Judge of the Miners Court He the Judge shall be entitled to a fee of two dollars in each, and every case, so comming, and in all cases the fees must be paid in advance by the Party or Parties instituting Suit. If the Party or Parties are not satisfied with the descision of Said Judge, Then the Party or Parties may take an appeal from the descision of said Judge to a Jury of six citizens of said Destrict, whose descision shall be final.

18th Resolved,

The Judge of the Miners Court Shall be entitled to a fee of one dollar for each summons or subena He may issue from His Office.

19th Resolved,

The Sheriff of this Destrict shall be entitled to a fee of One dollar for every summons or subena He may serve, and a fee of fifty cents on each Juror.

20th Resolved,

The Jury when summoned shall be entitled to one [dollar?] each, the Complainant in all cases arising pay the Cost ecruing in advance, but upon the final descision being rendered then the costs to be made out of the defeated Party or Parties.

21st Resolved,

All cases may be tried in five days after a summons may isue, and the Judge may hold His court on any Monday.

22d Resolved,

The Sheriff shall on Judgement being rendered final make His Levy, and advertize Property in three Publick Places in Said Destrict, and expose said property for sale at Publick Auction in Ten days after Such Levy having been made, to the highest and best Bidder.

LAWS REGULATING CLAIMS FOR RANCHING PURPOSES

23d Resolved,

That any one Individual can take up, and claim one hundred and sixty acres of land for ranching purposes, and any one Individual may take up, and claim one hundred and sixty acres of Land for each member of a company He may represent by representing the names of the company He may represent, and staking the land so taken and claimed with the names of the Party or Parties staking, and claiming which must be filed with the recorder of this Destrict for Record in five days after taken or claimed.

24th Resolved,

That all persons working a Lode by Tunnel shall be entitled to two hundred feet on each Side of Said Tunnel that said Tunnel may in its course pass Lodes in its course if so the Party or Parties constructing said Tunnell shall be entitled to two hundred feet on each Lode it may pass—each Side of said Tunnel—but must not interfere with any vested rights.

25th Resolved,

That any member of a company may represent the claims of the company and said claims shall be represented and worked within three months from the time such claim or claims are filed for record but any company working one claim shall hold without working all other claims that they may have in this District.

26th Resolved,

That all water claims or mill sites shall be held unimproved for Twelve Months from the time such claim or claims are taken and filed for Record.

Griffith Mining District, 22 Sept. 1860

At a meeting of the miners of the Griffith District held on the 22d day of September 1860 acording to previous notice when Jilson Ray was called to the Chair and Geo. F. Griffith acting as secretary when the following resolutions were adopted.

Resolved 1st. That all Water Mill and Mining Claims now taken claimed and Recorded hereafter shall be held without improvement until the tenth (10th) day of July A.D. eighteen hundred and sixty one (1861)

Resolved 2d. That any person or persons discovering lodes of quarts gold/silver or other valuable minerals shall be entitled to two hundred (200) feet in length on the course of the lode and twenty five feet on each side of the center of the quartz or mineral crevis [crevice] on each and every lode he or they may discover.

Resolved 3rd. That all and every discovery claim now taken staked and recorded or that may be taken staked and recorded hereafter shall be held exempt from execution or attachment.

Resolved 4. That any person or persons taking and claiming lode claims in this District shall be entitled to hold and work any and all quarts valuable metals and minerals of any and all kinds whatsoever embraced within the limits of his or their claims of fifty [feet?] in width by one hundred (100) feet in length Measuring twenty five (25) feet each side of the center of the quarts or mineral crevis and no person or persons shall lawfully enter upon any part or parcel of such claim or claims for the purpose of digging or mining without the consent of the proper owner or owners.

Resolved 5th. That Resolution ninth of the laws of this District be so amended as to read as follows, That all lode claims shall be no more than one hundred (100) feet in length on the course of the lode and twenty five feet on each side of the center of the quarts or mineral crevis.

Resolved 6th. That no persons or persons shall take or cause to be taken from this District into another District any wood square or building timber or logs of any kind and any person or persons so transgressing shall be fined the sum of fifty (50.) Dollars for the first offense and double that amount for every other offence one half of such fines to go to informant and one half to the benefit of the District. Such fines to be collected as provided in civil suits.

No other business coming befor the meeting they adjourned *sine die*.

Geo. F. Griffith
Secretary

Jilson Ray
Chairman

Griffith District Jan 12th 1861

At a meeting of the miners of the Griffith Mining District held at the office of the Recorder of said District according to previous notice when James Burrell was called to the chair and Geo. F. Griffith acting as secretary When the following Resolutions were adopted.

Resolved 1st. That any person or persons legal voters of this District may call a meeting of the miners of the District for any purpose or purposes whatever by tendering the Recorder of said District the sum of ($2.00) Two dollars it shall then be the duty of the Recorder to call such meeting by posting three different notices in three different conspicuous places in the district said notices to specify the time place and object of said meeting said notices to be posted at least five (5) days in advance of said meeting.

Resolved 2d. That any person holding a claim in this district which is duly Recorded in the books of the District shall be considered a legal voter in all affairs and meetings of this District.

Resolved 3rd. That any officer or officers of this District absenting themselves from this District for the space of (60) sixty days shall forfeit their office and the same shall be declared vacant And any officer about to quit the District for a space of time shall appoint a Deputy to act in his absence.

Resolved 4th. That any office or offices in this District becoming vacant a miners meeting may be called by the Resident Voters of the District and at said meeting said vacancy or vacancies shall be filled by the election of officers to fill the vacancy for the unexpired term of said office or offices.

Resolved 5th. That all purchase claims the Deed or Transfer of which is duly recorded in the Books of the District shall be held as real estate.

Resolved 6th. That any claim or claims entered upon the Records of this District the certificates of which have not been issued nor the fees for recording the same paid over at the expiration of the term of (60) sixty days from the date of Recording the same shall be sold at public auction by the Recorder of the District and the Moneys accrueing from said sale after the reduction of the Recorders fees and the expences of said sale shall revert to the District for the benefit of the same The Recorder shall give at least ten days notice of the sale of such claims by posting the notices in three different conspicuous places in the District.

Resolved 7th. That a committee of three be apointed to measure the water or mill priveleges in this District and number the same in rotation commencing at the lower end of the District and that said committee report at a meeting to be called on the 26th twenty sixth day of January A D 1861.

Resolved 8th That Messrs Geo F Griffith James Burrell and W L Gibson form said committee.

Resolved 9th. That it be the duty of the sheroff of this District to enforce Resolution (6th) sixth of the Resolutions passed at a meeting held Sept 22nd A D 1860 taking such mesures for the enforcement of said Resolution as will prove effective.

Resolved 10th. That all votes for offices this District shall be By Ballot and that the president and Recorder be the Bord of Canvassers for all such elections.

Resolved 11th. That the President Recorder and sheroff of this District shall be required to give good and sufficient security in the sum of one hundred dollars the bonds of the President to be approved by the Recorder and the bonds of the Recorder and Sheroff to be approved by the President.

Resolved 12th. That the officers of this District shall be duly qualified and sworn in the following manner The Recorder of this District shall qualify the President and sheroff and the President shall qualify the Recorder.

On motion preceded to the election of officers to fill vacancies for the unexpired term when James Burrell was elected president and Cyrus Hiltabiddle was elected Sheroff. No other business coming before the meeting adjourned until Jan 26th 1861.

Geo F. Griffith — Secretary
James Burrell — Chairman

This adjourned meeting from Jan. 12th 1861 met according to adjournment at the office of the Recorder of this the Griffith District on Jan. 26th 1861

When the Committee apointed to measure and number the water or mill claims of said District submitted the following report which was unanimously received and adopted as follows to wit:

Whereas the water or mill claims of this the Griffith Mining District were not regularly measured and marked and likely in future to cause trouble and litigation and whereas we the undersigned were at a meeting duly called on the 12th day of Jan. 1861 apointed a committee to measure and number said claims commencing at the lower end of said District

Therefore your committee begs leave to submit the following Report to wit:

Your committee commenced acording to instruction and measured up the South Clear Creek to the junction of the West and South forks of said stream and found seventy one claims (71) sixty nine of which are full claims of three hundred (300) feet each and two (2) fractional claims nineteen (19) and seventy one (71) nineteen containing two hundred and forty one (241) feet and seventy one (71) containing one hundred and forty two (142) feet and preempted according to the Records of said District as follows to wit: No. 1 Bates Nos. 2-3-4 Harding & Co. No. 5 Ray Nos. 6-7-8 Simmons & Co. No. 9 Leavenworth No. 10 Burrell No. 11 Coulson No. 12 Coulson No. 13 Wooden No. 14 Crawford No. 15 Russell No. 16 Davis No. 17 King No. 18 Soggs No. 19-20 Jones & Co. Nos. 21-22-23-24-25-26-27-28-29-30-31-32 South Clear Creek Mining Co. Nos. 33-34-35-36 Mitchell & Co. No. 37 Hiltabiddle No 38 Fellows No. 39 Griffith No. 40 Griffith Nos. 41-42-43-44-45-46-47-48-49-51-52-53-54-55 vacant No. 56-57 Cook & Co. Nos. 58-59-60 Darling & Co. Nos. 61-62-63-64 Gibson & Co. Nos. 65-66-67 Pierce & Co. Nos. 68-69-70-71 Queen & Co. Also your Committee measured up the South and West forks of said stream and finding them preempted acording to the Records of said District as follows to wit:

West fork of South Clear Creek Nos. 1-2-3-4-5 Hornes and Co. No. 6 Tush No. 7 Shurber No. 8 Barker No. 9 Griffith No.

10 Renshaw No. 11 Griffith No. 12-13-14 Laramer & Co. No. 15-16 Griffith Geo F. No. 17 Gooding No. 18 Burrell No. 19 Leavenworth

South fork of South Clear Creek No. 1 Griffith Nos. 2-3-4-5 Chapeze & Co. Nos. 6-7-8 Griffith & Co. Nos. 9-10-11-12-13 Mitchell & Co. Nos. 14-15-16-17-18 Quaintance & Co. No. 19 Sweney No. 20 Case

Geo. F. Griffith

James Burrell

No other business being before the Meeting they adjourned Sine Die

James Burrell
President

Geo. F Griffith Sec.

The miners met pursuant to call March 2d 1861 President presiding Geo F Griffith acting as secretary When the following Resolutions were adopted

Resolved 1st That this meeting as per call of Recorder appoint a committee to confer with a committee from the Union District appointed for the purpose of Defineing and establishing Territorial Boundries Between this and said District to consist of Geo F. Griffith James Burrell and W L Gibson and Report at a meeting of the miners at the Recorders office on Saturday March 9th at 9. oclock A M 1861 and also to report permanent boundries for this District

Resolved 2d. That this meeting appoint a committee consisting of James Burrell D.T. Griffith and Henry Chapeze to codify and revise the Laws governing this District and report at a meeting of the miners Saturday 9 oclock A.M March 9th 1861

Resolved 3rd. That all timber to be used for House logs must be used within ten days after felling the same unless it be shown that some unavoidable accident prevented the requirements of this section.

Resolved 4th. That all saw logs shall be hauled to the mill site for which they are intended within thirty days from the time of felling the same and they must trimed and marked at the time of felling

Resolved 5th. That no party or parties shall be allowed to fell timber for Saw Logs until they have their mill machinery on the ground and are using ordinary diligence toward the erection of the same

Resolved 6th. That any and all timber now lying upon the ground in the tree [District?] shall be forfeited within the space of thirty days from this date by public notice being given by posters being posted in three principal points in this district after the expiration of said time said timber shall become common property of the District and be governed as standing timber acording to Resolution (5th) fifth of the Resolutions and no person shall convert or change the condition of said fallen timber until they comply with said resolution No (5) five.

No other Business the meeting adjourned to meet on Saturday March 9th at 9 oct. A.D 1861

James Burrell President
Geo F Griffith Secretary

The miners met pursuant to adjournment March the 9th at 9 oclock A M. A D 1861 when the following committee Reports and Resolutions were submited and adopted

Report of Committee On Boundary Line Between Union And Griffith Districts

The Commissioners appointed to establish the Boundry and Dividing Line between Union and Griffith Districts agree as follows to witt Beginning at a point upon the West line of Montana District due East from the cone of Douglas Mountain Thence West to said cone and along the Main Ridge of Said Mountain through Union pass and along the Summit of Columbian Mountain Westerly as far as the West Line of Union District about seven miles

March 4th 1861

Commissioners from Griffith District	Geo. F. Griffith W L Gibson James Burrell
Commissioners from Union District	Geo L Nicholls N D Short

Report of Committee On Permanent Boundaries

We the committee appointed for the purpose of Defineing and Establishing the entire Boundry lines for this District beg leave to Submit the following The Boundries of this District Shall commence at a point on the West Line of Montana District due East from the cone of Douglas Mountain Thence West to said Cone and along the Main Ridge of said mountain through Union pass and along the summit of the Columbian [-Mountain-] to the Democrat Mountain thence along the summit of the same to the Republican Mountain thence along the summit of said mountain to a point on said summit opposite a point on West Branch three miles above its junction with the South Branch of South Clear Creek Thence in a South Easterly direction to a point on the said South Branch three miles above said junction Thence East to the summit of the mountain side of said South Branch thence North to the Summit of Independent Hill thence along the summit of said Hill until said Boundry Line May reach a point on the West line of Montana District thence North to the place of Beginning

Resolved 1st. That the Recorder is hereby authorized to copy the original laws of this District into a Book to be kept for the purpose Except such as are repealed by the Revised Laws adopted Mar 9th A D 1861 and that he be allowed a reasonable compensation for the same to be paid from any moneys in the treasury not otherwise appropriated also to copy the Revised Laws in the same book

No other business comeing before the Meeting they adjourned Sine Die

Geo F Griffith	James Burrell
Secretary	President

Decleration of the Returns of an Election held in this District as per call of President March 16th 1861 for the purpose of Electing officers of this District for the ensuing year consisting of one President & Judge of the Miners Court one Recorder one Sheroff and one Surveyor who having been voted for according to the Election Laws of this District Resulted as follows James Burrell having received the greatest number of votes for the office of President & Judge of the Miners Court was declared duly elected

Geo F Griffith having received the greatest number of votes for the office of Recorder was declared duly elected

P Mclain haveing received the greatest number of votes for the office of Sheriff was declared duly elected.

D T Griffith having received the greatest number of votes for the office of Surveyor was declared duly elected

We the undersigned Board of Election do hereby certify that the above are true and correct returns

Griffith Mining District
March 16th 1861

J S Griffith George Marshall	} Judges
Geo F Griffith D T Griffith	} Clerks

Griffith Mining District Mar 26th 1861

Old Laws unrepealed by the Revised Laws enacted for this District March 9th 1861____________________

Sept. 22d 1860

Resolved 1st That all water Mill and Mineing Claims now taken Claimed and Recorded that may be Taken and Recorded hereafter shal be held without improvement until the tenth (10th) day of July 1861________________

Resolved 4th That any person or persons Taking and Claiming Lode Claims in this District shal be entitled to hold and work any and all Quartz Valuable Mettals and Minerals of any kind watsoever embraced within the Limits of his or Their Claims of Fifty feet in Width by One Hundred feet in Length. Measuring (25) Twenty-five feet Each Side of the Center of the Quartz or Mineral Crevice and no person or persons shal Lawfully enter upon any part or parcel of such Claim or Claims for the purpose of Digging or Mining without the consent of the proper Owner or Owners________

Resolved 6th That no person or persons shal Take or Cause to be Taken from this District into an other District any wood Square or Building Timber or Logs of any kind And any person or persons so Transgressing shal be fined the Sum of Fifty Dollars for the First Offense and Double that amount for ever other offense One Half of such fines to go to the informant and one Half to the Benefit of the District such fines to be collected as provided in Civil Suits________________

Jany 12th 1861

Resolved 6th That any Claim or Claims entered upon the Records of this District the Certificates of which have not been issued nor the Fees for Recording the Same paid over at the expiration of (60) Sixty days from the Date of Recording the Same Shal be sold at Public Auction by the Recorder of the District and the Monies accruing from said sale after the Reduction of the Recorders fees and the Expenses of Said Sale Shal revert to the District for the Benefit of the Same. The Recorder shal give at Least Ten days Notice of the Sale of such Claims by posting three Notices in Three Conspicuous places in the District__________________

Resolved 9th

That it be the duty of the Sheriff of this District to enforce Resolution (6th) Sixth of the Resolutions passed at a Meeting held Sept 22d AD 1860 taking such Measures for the enforcement of said Resolution as will prove effective________________

March 2d 1861

Resolved 1st

That this meeting as per call of the Recorder appoint a Committee to confer with a Committee from the Union District appointed for the purpose of Defining and establishing the Territorial Boundaries between this and Said District to Consist of Geo. F. Griffith James Burrell and W.S. Gibson, And Report at a Meeting of the Miners at the Recorders office on Saturday Mar. the 9th @ 9 ocl" AM 1861, And also report permanent Boundaries for this District______________

Resolved 2d

That this Meeting appoint a Committee consisting of James Burrell D.T. Griffith Henry Chapeze to Codify and Review the Laws governing this District and Report at a Meeting of the Miners Saturday 9 ocl" AM March 9th 1861__________________

Resolved 3rd

That all timber to be used for House Logs Must be used within ten days after filing the same unless it be shown that some unavoidable accident prevented the fulfillment of the Requirements of this Section___________________

Resolved 4th

That all saw Logs shal be hauled to the Mill Site for which they are intended within thirty days from the time of felling the Same and they must be trimmed and marked at the time of felling

Resolved 5th

That no party or parties shal be allowed to fell timber for saw Logs until they have their mill machinery upon the ground and are using ordinary diligence toward the Erection of the Same

Resolved 6th

That any and all timber now lying upon the ground in this trio [?] shall be forfeited within the space of thirty days from this date by public notice being given by posters hung posted in three principal points in this District After the Expiration of said time Said timber shal become Common property of the District and be governed as standing timber according to Resolution (5th) Fifth of these Resolutions and no person shall convert or change the condition of said fallen timber until they comply with said Resolution No. (5) five

Report of Committee to Confer with Union

March 9th 1861

The Commissioners appointed to Establish the Boundaries and Dividing Line between Union and Griffith Districts agree as folows to Wit"

Beginning at a point upon the West line of Montanna District and East from the Cone of Douglas Mountain. Thence West to said Cone and along the Main Ridge of Said Mountain Through Union Pass and along the Summit of Columbian Mountain Westerly as far as the West Line of Union District about Seven Miles.

March 4th 1861	Geo. F. Griffith
Commissioners from Griffith District	James Burrell W S Gibson
Commissioners from Union District	Geo. L. Nickolls W D Short

Report of Committee on Permanent Boundaries

We the Committee appointed for the purpose of Defining and Establishing permanent Boundaries Lines for this District Beg Leave to submit the folowing.

The Boundaries of this District shal commence at a point on the West line of Montanna District due East from the Cone of Douglas Mountain. Thence West to said Cone and along the Main Ridge of Said Mountain through Union Pass and along the Summit of the Columbian to the Democrat Mountain thence along the Summit of the Same to the Republican Mountain thence along the Summit of Said Mountain to a point on Said Summit opposite a point on West Branch Three Miles above its Junction with the South Branch of South Clear Creek Thence in a South Easterly direction to a point on the Said South Branch three miles above its Junction Thence East to the Summit of the Mountain Side of Said South Branch thence North to the Summit of Independent Hill thence along the Summit of Said Hill until Said Boundary Line May Reach a point on the West Line of Montanna District thence North to the place of Begining

Geo. F. Griffith
Committee James Burrell

Resolved"

That the Recorder is hereby authorized to coppy the original Laws of this District into a Book to be kept for that purpose except such as are Repealed by the Revised Lws addopted Mar 9th 1861. And that he be allowed a reasonable Compensation for the Same to be paid from any Monies in the treasury not otherwise appropriated

Also to Coppy the Revised Laws in Same Book

Election Returns

Declaration of the Returns of an Election held in this District (as per Call of the President) March the 16th 1861 for the purpose of Electing officers for this District for the Ensuing Year. Consisting of one President and Judge of the Miners Court, One Recorder, One Sheriff and one Surveyor, Who having been Voted for according to the Election Laws of this District Results as folows

James Burrell. Having Received the greatest Number of Votes for the Office of President and Judge of the Miners Court was Declared duly Elected.

Geo. F. Griffith. Having received the greatest number of Votes for the office of Recorder was Declared duly Elected.

J.M. Lain Having Received the greatest Number of Votes for the Office of Sheriff was declared duly elected.

D.T. Griffith Having Received the Greatest Number of Votes for the Office of Surveyor was declared duly Elected.

We the Undersigned Board of Election do hereby Certify that the above are True and Correct Returns

District Mining District
March 16th 1861

John S. Griffith
Geo Marshall } Judges

Geo. F. Griffith
D.T. Griffith } Clerks

Filed and Recorded March 16th 1861.
Geo. F. Griffith
Recorder

Report of a Committee

Consisting of James Burrell, D. T. Griffith and H. Chapeze appointed March 2d 1861 for the purpose of codifying and Revising the Laws of this District Who Reported the folowing, which was addopted by a Miners' Meeting Held at the Recorders Office March the 9th 1861 ______________________

BOUNDARIES

Chapter 1st
Section 1st

The Boundries of this District shal Commence at a point on the West Line of Montanna District, due East from the Cone of the Douglas Mountain Thence West to Said Cone and along the Main Ridge of said Mountain through Union Pass and along the Summit of Columbian to the Democrat Mountain Thence along the Summit of the Same to the Republican Mountain Thence along the Summit of Said Mountain to a point on Said Summit oposite a point on West Branch Three Miles above its Junction with the

South Branch of South Clear Creek and Thence in a South Easterly direction to a point on the Said South Branch to a point Three Miles above Said Junction Thence East to the Summit of the Mountain on East Side of Said South Branch Thence North to the Summit of Independent Hill Thence along the Summit of Said Hill until Said Boundry Line May reach a point on the West Line of Montanna District Thence North to the Place of Begining________________

OFFICERS

Chap 2d

Sec 1st

The officers of this District shal consist of a President (who shal be Judge of the Miners' Court) a Sheriff a Surveyor and a Recorder who shal Ex eficio be Treasurer and Secretary of the District.

Which officers shal be Elected on the (3rd) Third Saturday of March of Each Year and hold their offices for the Term of One year from the date of their Election or until their Successors are Elected and quaified. Unless he sooner Die, Remove from the District, Resign or is Removed for Mis conduct as herinafter provided______________

Sec 2d

When any officer (except the President) of this District shal be guilty of Misconduct or Malfeasance in Office it shal be the Duty of the president When an affidivit is Made setting forth the Specific Charge, To Issue a Notice to such officer to appear before him for Trial. The President shal appoint a prosecutor and the Trial shal be conducted according to the Laws for Misdemeanor_____________

Sec. 3d

In case The President of the District is charged with Misconduct in office it shal be the duty of the Recorder to preform the duties prescribed for the President in the forgoing section___

Sec 4th

Each officer before entering upon the Duties of his office shal take an oath to support and faithfully execute all the Laws of this District______________

DUTIES OF OFFICERS

Duties of President

Chapter 3

Sec 1st

It shal be the duty of the President to preside at all Legaly called Meetings of the Miners and to call special Meetings by posting three Notices within the District at Least Three days before the Time of Said Meeting When in his opinion there is a necessity for the Same. Or when a petition is presented sighned by a majority of the Citizens specifying the particular object of the Meeting Which object Must be distinctly stated in the Notice

Sec 2d

It shal be the duty of the President to sighn all orders on the Treasurer for Money Legally appropriated and all Deeds for property belonging to the District which the Miners of the District authorize to be Sold. And also to have the Care of any property belong to the District except such as is the special duty of some other officer to protect

It shal also be his duty to institute suit against any person guilty of Destroying or injuring any property belonging to the District, or committing any offense Recognized in the Law as a Misdemeanor Nuisance or Crime and to appoint a sutable person to conduct the prosecution_________

Sec. 3d

It shal be the Duty of the President to appoint an officer Protem to fill any vacancy that may occur until such vacancy can be filled by a Regular Called Election__________

DUTIES OF JUDGE

Chapter 4th
Sec 1st

The Judge of the Miners' Court shal Execute a Bond with good and Sufficient security to be approved by the Recorder in the penal sum of $500 Five Hundred Dollars for the faithful performance of his duties______________

Sec 2d

The Miners' Court shal have jurisdiction over all Civil Contracts Made in this or any other District in Colorado Territory provided the parties are Citizens of this District at the time of Making the Contract or provided the Defendent is a Citizen of this District at the time of the institution of the Suit________

Sec 3d

It shal be the duty of the Judge in all Cases before entering suit to Require a Bond of Good and Sufficient security for the payment of all costs, and for all Damages in case of attachment being wrongfully sued out And also Require of Boath Plaintiff and Defendant in any suit prepayment of Costs before the Rendition of Judgement such Costs to be Refunded to the party gaining the Suit, The adverse party paying all costs______________

Sec 4th

No Suit shal be brought in the Miners Court for indebtedness contracted in any other State or Territory except by consent of all parties interested, And No Execution shal be colectable on Judgement rendered upon such indebtness except as hereinbefore provided___________

Sec 5th

The Judge of the Miners Court shal keep a Docket upon which a Correct record of all the proceedings of his Court shal be kept, And he shal file and Safely Keep all papers Connected with Suits before him___________

Sec 6th

It shal be the Duty of the Court to Levy a fine not to exceed Ten Dollars for Contempt of Court. Said fine to be collected by Sale of property on Execution and the proceeds of the Same to be paid into the District Treasury__________

Sec 7

It shal be the Duty of the Judge to Issue an attachment when the Plaintiff in any Suit Shal Make oath that he believes the Defendant is about to abscond or dispose of his property to Defraud his creditors_____________

Sec 8th

The Judge of the Miners' Court shall have ful probate jurisdiction within this District____________

Sec 9

It shal be the Duty of the Judge of the Miners Court to pay over to the Treasurer of the District all Monies Coming into his hands for fines___________

DUTIES OF RECORDER

Chapter 5th

Sec 1st

It Shal be the Duty of the Recorder safely to Keep the Records of the District and to Record all papers upon the payment of his fees. To act as secretary at all public Meetings of the District. And by Virtue of his office as Treasurer to Keep all Monies of the District paid to him subject to the Drafts of the President. Also to Keep all vouchers so that at any time he May be able when Called upon to Exibit the financial Conditions of the District____

Sec 2d

The Recorder May appoint a Deputy who shal be duly sworn for whose special acts he shal be Responsible___________

Sec 3d

It shal be the duty of the Recorder to execute a Bond with good and Sufficient security in the penal sum of ($500) Five

Hundred Dollars to be approved by the President and Judge of the District for the faithful performance of the Duties of his office__

DUTIES OF SHERIFF

Chapter 6th
Sec 1
The Sheriff of the District shal execute a Bond with good and sufficient security to be approved by the President and Judge of the District in the Penal Sum of ($500) Five Hundred Dollars for the faithful preformance of the Duties of his office.

Sec 2d
It shal be the duty of the Sheriff to Execute all papers issued by the proper officers and Make due returns entered thereon__

Sec 3d
It shal be the duty of the Sheriff to return any Notice or Summons on or before the time set therein for trial and the Manner of Service shal be set forth in the Sheriffs return thereto______

Sec 4th
It shal be the duty of the Sheriff when he attaches any property not Capable of Manuel Delivery to file a List of the Same with the Recorder immediately___________

Sec 5th
It shall be the Duty of the Sheriff to receive and return in person all papers which it is his duty to serve and Execute and to be present at all sittings of the Court and to preform such other duties as May be required of him by Law______________

DUTIES OF SURVEYOR

Chapter 7th
Sec 1st
It shal be the duty of the *Surveyor* of the District to Stake and Level Claims when called upon to do so by any person upon the payment of his fees. To decide all questions of Measurement be-

tween parties. And to Survey Stake and plat all building Lots within this District_______________

OFFICERS FEES

Chapter 8th

Sec 1st

The *Judge* of the Miners Court shal be allowed (50c) Fifty Cents each for issuing all papers except Subpoenas for which he shal receive (25c) Twenty five Cents if Containing one name and (50c) if containing More than one Name. For Docket Entries ($1.00) One Dollar. For Trial of Each Cause ($1.50) One Dollar and Fifty Cents. For Each Continuance of a Cause ($1.00) One Dollar_________

Sec 2d

The Recorder shal be entitled to (50c) Fifty Cents for Recording Each Claim (50c) Fifty Cents for a Deed or any instrument of Not More than one Hundred Words and at the Rate of (50c) fifty Cents for Each additional 100 Words___________

Sec 3d

The Sheriff Shal receive the Sum of (50c) Each for Serving all papers except Subpoenas for which he shal be entitled to (25c) for each person subpoenaed. When on official Business outside of the District he Shal be allowed 10c for Each Mile Necessarily Traveled.

He shal also be allowed 50c Each for those Notices in Case of sale under Execution and $1.00 one Dollar for Selling property. For Empanneling a Jury of Six ($1.00) one Dollar. For Summoning a Jury for a Regular Term of Court ($1.50) One Dollar and Fifty Cents. For Waiting on the Court 50c for Each Cause tried_________

Sec 4th

The Surveyor Shal receive (50c) Fifty Cents for Each Building Lot Surveyed Staked and Platted to be paid out of any Money in the District Treasury Not otherwise appropriated. And he shal receive ($5.00) Five Dollars per day for Staking and Surveying

Claims and Deciding Questions of Measurement between parties to be paid by the parties requesting the Same_________

Sec 5th

Jurors Shal each be allowed (50c) Fifty Cents an hour from the Setting of the Court until Dismissal of the Jury_________

Sec 6th

Witnesses Shal be allowed ($1.00) one Dollar for Each attendance upon a Cause which shal be paid in advance if Required_____________

LAWS FOR THE MINNERS COURT

Capter 9

Sec 1st

Regular Terms of the Miners Court shal be held on the (1st) first and (3d) third Tuesdays of Each Month and all writs to be Made Returnable at any Term shal be served and Returned on or before the Saturday preceding said Term. Provided that Nothing herin Contained shal be so construed as to prevent trials of crime or misdeanor at any time___________

Sec 2d

Any person wishing to commence a Civil action in the Miner's Court shal file with the Judge of said Court a statement in writing setting forth the grounds of Complaint which shal contain all the allegations and facts necessary to constitute a cause of action in Plain unequivocal Language And if the Defendant does not appear and answer to Said Complaint, The Court shall require Plantiff to Make oath to the Correctness of his complaint and that he knows of no Legal offset which the Defendant May have. Upon complying with the foregoing requirements the Judge may enter judgement for the ammount Claimed together with all Costs of Suit________

Sec 3d

Depositions May be used in evidence before the Miners Court provided the Witness is sick and unable to attend at the place of trial, About to leave the Country or is out of the jurisdiction of the Court. Provided also that the adverse party shal have notice of the time and place when and where such Depositions will be taken. And then have the right to Cross question such Witness. Notice however Need not be given when the Witness is not a Resident of this Territory___________

Sec 4th

No Cause shal be continued Except by consent of Boath parties or upon the affidavit of one of the parties or his attorney setting forth good cause for Continuance, or for the abscence of a Material Witness in which case the partys shal state on oath that he cannot safely proceed to trial without said Witness and that he believes that he can procure the testimony of said Witness at some specified time___________

Sec 5th

Garnishee process may issue as a part of the original writ to be served upon boath the Defendent and garnisheer [?] or Separately or may be issued after Execution is returned unsatisfied And in Either Case if the Garnishee shal pay the Defendant the ammount of his indebtedness after Service of said Notice and before the final Judgement (if any is obtained) is paid he shal be liable to the Plantiff for Such Indebtedness___________

Sec 6th

The Jury for each term of the Court shal be drawn on the Thursday Next preceeding Each term in the folowing Manner. The Recorder shal furnish the Names of (25) twenty five good and Lawful Men Citizens of the District which names shall be placed in a Box kept for that purpose, from which the Recorder shal draw (9) Nine Names. Who shal be summoned by the Sheriff to serve as Jurors for the Next succeeding Term. But no person shal be compelled to Serve on the Jury for two succeeding terms________

Sec 7

New Trials May be granted for good Cause Shown according to the Rules of Common Law, provided the party applying for a New Trial first pay all costs that have already accrued___________

Sec 8th

It shal be optional with the parties to any suit wheather the Same Shal be tried by the JUDGE of the Miner's Court or by JURY____

Sec 9th

When Either party require a Jury it shal be the Duty of the Sheriff to Draw from the Box the Number required. And if for Cause or preemptory Chalange the Regular pannel is exhausted it shal be his duty to Summon others until the pannel is full__________

Sec 10th

The Regular Number of Jury Men to try Civil Causes unless otherwise agreed upon by the parties shal be three_________

Sec 11th

Each party shal have the right to three preemptory Chalanges and as Many as necessary for Cause_____________

Sec 12th

Appeals Either party feeling agrieved May apeal from a Decission of a Jury of three or the Judge to a jury in number not exceeding twelve. such number to be agreed upon by the parties____

Sec 13th

In Cases where an appeal is taken as provided in the foregoing section, the Case shal be Cited to the next term of Court to which the appeal is taken, provided at least Five days elapse between the time of taking such appeal and the Next Regular Term of the Court to which the appeal is taken. Unless otherwise agreed upon by the parties_______________

NOTICE

Chapter 10th

Sec 1st

Notice Shal be considered served when read to the party or parties or by leaving a Copy of the same at the Usual place of Residence when not to be found within the District___________

Sec 2d

Attachments shal be considered served by being read to the parties together with a List of the property attached. And in Case the party or parties cannot be found within the District, By Leaving a Copy of the Same at their usual place of Residence_____

Sec 3d

All Executions Issued from the Miner's Court shal be made returnable within twelve days from their Date and the Sheriff shall Note on Each Execution the Day and hour of receiving the same and return the Said execution within the twelve days whether satisfied or not with his official acts endorsed thereon__________

Sec 4th

Any property sold Under execution shal be advertised by posting Notices in three Conspicuous places in the District at Least Five days previous to the day of Sale said Notices must Designate the day and Hour of Sale Together with the Description of the property to be offered for Sale. The Sheriff may adjourn the sale to some future day, within the time specified for the Return of the Execution Provided there are no bids, or the bids are Unreasonably Low. Notice of such postponement shal be given during the Hours of sale___________________

PUBLICATION

Chapter 11th

Sec 1st

When Suit is instituted against any person who is absent from or a Non Resident of this District service May be had by posting Notices or Coppies of the Summons in three Conspicuous places in the District at Least ten days previous to the day of trial. A Copy of one of Said Notices shal be sworn to by the Sheriff who posted the Same stating When How and Where he served the Same which shal be filed with the papers in the Case.

Sec 2d

When Judgement is rendered upon Publication as provided in the foregoing section the party Defendent shal be entitled to a new hearing in the Said Cause within (60) Sixty days after the Rendition of Judgement, By paying all Costs as showing to the Satisfaction of the Court, That injustice has been done him in the Case and in Case the Judgment is reversed, He shal be entitled to Receive any Property or its Value which May of been Sold in Execution of Such Judgement.

EQUITY

Chapter 12th

Sec 1st

The Miner's Court shal have Equity Jurisdiction, And shal be governed by Common Law Rules of Equity. Provided Either party shal have the right to trial by Jury, and provided either party shal show to the Satisfaction of Court that he cannot obtain Justice under the Rules of Law______________

EXEMPTION

Chapter 13th

Sec 1st

There shal be exempt from Levy and Sale upon Execution the folowing articles which are Necessary for present use by the Defendent: Mining Tools, Mechanics Tools, Reading, Clothing, Cooking Utensils, Necessary Provisions for three Months. One Claim so Designated on the Records And in Case of a Man of a Family Residing in the District a Dwelling house not Exceeding ($300) Three Hundred Dollars in Value and the Lot upon which the Same is situated. Together with such articles of Household Furniture as are Strictly Necessary. Provided that Nothing in the section shal apply to judgement rendered for Labor or Wages performed previous to this Date__________________

REDEMPTION

Chapter 14th

Sec 1st

The Defendent in any Cause on which Suit is not already Commenced shal have the right of Redemption on any Property Sold on Execution by paying to the Court for the Benefit of the purchaser in the amount of the purchase Money together with interest at the Rate of (5%) five per cent per Month if paid within (60) days from said sale________________

CITIZENSHIP

Chapter 15th

Sec 1st

Any Male person Eighteen Years of age haveing resided in this District (10) days Next preceeding an election or Miners Meeting shal be entitled to Vote and to all the Rights of Citizenship____

CRIMINAL LAWS

Sec 1st

Any person guilty of wilful murder upon conviction thereof shal be hung by the Neck Until he is dead_____________

Sec 2d

Any person guilty of Manslaughter or Homecide shal be punished as a Jury of twelve Men May Direct__________

Sec 3rd

Any person Shooting or Threatening to Shoot an other. Using or threatening to use any Deadly Weapons except in self Defence shal be fined in a Sum not Less than ($50) Fifty nor more than ($500) Five Hundred Dollars and receive in addition as Many stripes on his bare Back as a Jury of (6) Six Men May direct and be Banished from the District____________

Sec 4th

Petit Larceny Any person found guilty of Petit Larceny shal be fined in a Sum Double the Amount Stolen and Such other Punishment as a Jury of Six Men May Direct_____________

Sec 5th

Grand Larceny Any person found guilty of grand Larceny shal be fined in a Sum Double the Amount Stolen and receive as many lashes on his bare back as a Jury of Six Men May Direct and be Banished from the District________________

Sec 6th

Forgery Any person found guilty of forging Deeds, Transfers, Bills of Sale or Jumping Claims Legally held upon the Record Defacing Names, or Removing Stakes from their proper places, shal pay a fine of ($5) Five Dollars for Each offence and Double the amount of Damages Sustained by the Injured party. Said Damages to be determined by a Jury of Six Men________________

Sec 7th

Nuisance Any person who shal cause or commit any Nuisance affecting or Liable to affect the health of the people of this District upon Conviction thereof shal pay a fine not Exceeding ($100) One Hundred Dollars to be determined by a Jury of Six Men and Remove such Nuisance within a Reasonable time such time to be Determined by a Jury of Six Men________________

Sec 8th

Any person convicted of causing a Nuisance and failing or Refusing to Remove the Same Shal suffer the Same penalty (as prescribed in section Seven of this Chapter) for Each succeeding day after the Expiration of the time Required to Remove the same and such other punishment as a Jury May Direct______________

Sec 9th

All and every offence not inummerated in the foregoing sections shal be Determined by a Jury of Six Men and punished as they May Direct________________

Sec 10th

Larceny Defined Any theft not exceeding Ten Dollars in Value shal be Deemed Petit Larceny. And any theft over that sum in value shal be Deemed Grand Larceny_____________

CLAIMS DEFINED

Chapter 17th

Sec 1st

The term Claim used in this District shal be construed to Mean when applied to a Lode (100ft) One Hundred feet extending the length of the Same and (25 ft) Twenty five feet on Each side from Center of Crevice. Unless thereby interfering with an other Lode When an Equitable Divission of Territory shal be Made___________

When applied to a Gulch (100 ft) in Length on the Same and (50 ft) Fifty feet in Width______________

When applied to Patch or placer Diggins (100 ft) One Hundred feet Square______

When applied to Tunnel Claims the entire distance intended to Run the Same as shown by the Record and Stake at the Mouth of the Tunnel Together with the Surface grounds for Deposits as hereinafter provided______________

When applied to a Watter or Mill priviledge (300 ft) on the Creek or Gulch with the priveledge of using the watter of the Same And Mill Grounds adjacent thereto (150 ft) Each side of the Creek or Gulch and More if Necessary for the enjoyment of the Same_______

When applied to a Ditch Claim the entire distance staked out which they intend to Run the Same as Shown by the Survey and Stakes_________________

When applied to a Creek Bed Mining Claim (100 ft) One Hundred feet up and down the Creek in Length and between high Watter Mark on Each Side______________

When applied to Bar Claims (50 ft) fifty feet in width Running Back to the Base of the Mountain________________

LAWS GOVERNING CLAIMS

Chapter 18th

Sec 1

All purchased Claims when Recorded shal be held as Real Estate______________

Sec 2d

No person shal hold more than one Claim on Each Lode, Creek, Bar, Patch or Gulch except by purchase or Discovery___________

Sec 3d

Any person Discovering a quartz Lode by Recording the Same may hold the Discovery Claim as Real Estate, and one other Claim by preemption on Said Lode________________

Sec 4th

All Quartz Lodes shal terminate in the Center of Each Creek___

Sec 5th

When Lode Claims extend through Bar Claims the first Claim Recorded shal [sic.] Hold Boath ____________

Sec 6th

Any person owning a Quartz Mill or Claim on which he has a Mill or is preparing to place a Mill, Shal have a right to cut or construct a Race, Flume or Ditch to Carry Watter to such Mill over any Claim Road or Ditch. Provided the watter be so guarded as not to interfere with vested Rights. Priority of Claims to be in every Case Respected__________________

Sec 7th

The Discovery Hole shal be considered the Center of the Discovery Claim unless specified to the Contrary on the Record____

Sec 8th

No person shal be allowed to Mine under any Building or other improvement unless they first secure the parties owning such Improvement against all Damages except by priority of title_______

Sec 9th

All Deeds, Bonds, Contracts, Bills of Sale or Instruments of any Kind Relating to the Conveyance of Property shal be witnessed and Must be Recorded within (30) thirty days after their Date to be held as valid against Creditors or Subsequent Deeds of Grantor__

Sec 10th

Preemptions on Lodes which Run into Each other shal be governed by the priority of the Discoveries______________

Sec 11th

In all cases when parties shal have complied with the Law as far as possible priorty of Claim and honestly carried out shal be Respected____________

TUNNEL LAW

Chapter 19th

Sec 1st

Any person or Company Locating or having Located a Tunnel Claim in this District as herinafter provided shal be entitled to One by Two Hundred feet of Ground as Surface Claim at the Starting point for tunnel purposes and Deposits____________

Sec 2d

Any person or Company owning a Tunnel under this Law shal be entitled to four Hundred feet and No More upon any Lode which said Tunnel May Cross two Hundred feet of which May be taken on Each Side of the Center Line of the Tunnel Claim provided Such Lode has not been Discovered and Claimed prior to the preempting of Said Tunnel and they shal have the exclusive right to all Quartz Minerals or Valuable Metals that May be found within the Boundaries of said Tunnel____________

Sec 3d

Any person or Company owning a Tunnel as aforesaid shal be required to commence work upon the Same on or before the 10th day of July Next in which Month he or they shal be required to preform ($50) Fifty Dollars Worth of Labor upon said Tunnel. After which he or they shal be required to preform at least three Months Work for one Laborer in Each Six Months. Upon failing to comply with any of the requirements in this Section the right to such Tunnel Claim shal be forfeited____________

Sec 4th

All Tunnel Claims shal be staked at the Starting points in the Center upon which stake shall be written the Direction and Terminus of Said Tunnel. Together with the name of the owner or owners____

Sec 5th

Any person or Company owning a Tunnel as aforesaid shall have the right to cross any Lode on the Line of said Tunnel provided the amount of Quartz taken out of Such Lode shal not be more than is necessary to cross said Lode holding the Size of Said Tunnel at smalest place____________

Sec 6th

Any person or Company owning Lode Claims through which a Tunnel under this Law may pass shal have the right either in person or by their agent to inspect such Lode claim in Said tunnel at any time they may desire__________

Sec 7th

When a person or Company Claims to have Discovered a New Lode in their Tunnel and Said Lode is Claimed by Discovery prior to Locating of said Tunnel, It shall devolve upon the Tunnel owner to show that his discovery is a new one_____________

Sec 8th

All persons owning Lode Claims shal have the privilege to work the Same by Tunnel or otherwise and to Deposit Quartz either by Slide or Tramway at the point most convenient for them on any ground not claimed under this Law for Surface Deposits______

Sec 9th

Any person or Company working one of His or their claims in this District shal hold thereby all the preempted Claims he or they may have in this District. Nothing herein to be so construed as to conflict with the Tunnel Law________________

LAW REGULATING LOTS

Chapter 20th

Sec 1st

Any person preempting Town Lots Within this District Must have the Same filed for Record the day of Taking the Same and Lay a foundation upon Said Lot which Shal Hold the Same for the Space of thirty Days. Then he or they shal build a house upon Said Lot within the Space of Sixty Days after the expiration of the foundation Stay. Then by paying the Recorder (in addition to his fees) the Sum of (50c) Fifty Cents Shal Receive a Deed from the president of the District for the Same. And in Case he or they fail to Comply with the above Laws said Lot shal be forfeited to the District__________________

INCORPORATIONS

Chapter 21st

Sec 1

Companies preempting Claims shal hold no more than there are Members of the Company Named as such upon the Record either in articles of incorporation or upon their Certificate________

ELECTION LAW

Chapter 22d

Sec 1st

All Elections for Officers of this District shal be by Ballot. And to be Conducted and held as follows. The Recorder and Sheriff Shal select from the Qualified Citizens of the District four persons who shal act as Judges and Clerks of the Election. Then after haveing been Qualified by the President in his abscence the Recorder, Shal take charge of the Polls. Receive, Sort, Count and Declare the Votes. Make proper Return thereof to the District by placing Said Returns in the hands of the Recorder for Record______

FILE LAW

Chapter 23rd

Sec 1

All claims filed for Record hold good for ten day before forfeiting the Claim Filed_____________

Any and all Laws Conflicting with the foregoing are hereby Repealed. Provided that Nothing herein Contained shal be so construed as to interfere with any rights acquired under previously existing Laws___________________

Enacted by the Miners of this District March the 9th AD 1861____________

Attest

James Burrell	President
Geo F Griffith	Recorder

Griffith Mining District

Miners met pursuant to call of the President of Apr 20th 1861

On Motion of D. T. Griffith the President was required to appoint a Committee for the purpose of Drafting a Lien Law and also a Law for the regulation of Mortgages and Report at a Meeting of the Miners to be held at the Recorders Office Apr 27th 1861

President appointed D.T. Griffith H K Pierson and J D Hall

On Motion D. T. Griffith the President appointed D. T. Griffith W. B. Squires and H B Snyder as a Committee for the purpose of Surveying Staking and Numbering the Water Claims on the South and West Branches of South Clear Creek also Leavenworth Creek and make their Report as soon as practable

On Motion D. T. Griffith The folowing Resolution and Laws were adopted

Resolved:

That we the Miners of this District do enact the folowing as Sections 11th and 12th of Chapter 16th of the Criminal Laws of this District

Sec 11th

Any Person or Persons found guilty of willfully or Maliciously rolling Stones (Quartz excepted) down hill upon any Mountain in this District Upon Conviction thereof shal pay a fine of not less than ($5) five nor over ($50) fifty Dollars to the District and Such other punishment as a Jury of 6 men may Direct

Sec 12th

Any person or persons found guilty of willfully or maliciously putting out fire or Setting fire to any Grass Timber or other combustable within the Limits of this District shal upon Conviction thereof pay a fine to the District of Not less than five nor over fifty Dollars and Receive such other punishment as a Jury of 6 men May Direct

On Motion Meeting adjourned to meet on Saturday Apr 27th.

Apr 20th 1861

Miners Met pursuant to adjournment this Apr 17th 1861

On Motion D. T. Griffith the folowing Resolutions and Laws were Unanimously adopted and Enacted

Resolved:

That that portion of Section 3a of Chapter 4th (of the Revised Laws) Immediately following the words sued out in the fifth Line of Said Section which relates to the Duty of Judge in requiring Prepayment of Costs Be and is hereby Repealed

Resolved:

That the following be and is hereby enacted and Shal be known as Section 6th of Chapter 6th of the Revised Laws of this District

Sec 6th of Chap 6th

It shal be the Duty of the Sheriff to execute or cause to be executed all penalties for criminal offense

Resolved:

That all timber now standing upon any town Lot within this District shal not be subject to appropriation by any person or persons except the Legal owners of said Lot or Lots. Also the timber now Standing upon Beaver Island (which is situated on the town site of Georgetown on Water Claims No 69 & 70) shal also be exempt from appropriation by any person whomsoever And any person found Guilty of Cutting felling or carrying away any such timber, shal Upon Conviction therof pay a fine to the District of Not less than ($5) fine nor over ($50) fifty Dollars and Such other punishment as a Jury May Direct

On Motion
Meeting adjourned to Meet Saturday May 4th
Griffith Mining District
Apr 27 1861

Saturday May 4th 1861. Miners Met pursuant to adjournment

The Committees appointed by the president at a Meeting held on Apr 20th 1861 not being ready to Make Report On Motion the Miners gave them more time.

On Motion D.T. Griffith the folowing Resolution was unanimously passed

Resolved:

That the words, "Within (30) days after their Date" of Section 9th of Chapter 18th of the Revised Laws of this District be and are hereby stricken out

On Motion Meeting adjourned to Meet Saturday May 11th at 7 ocl. PM

May 11th 1861 Miners Met pursuant to adjournment James Burrell presided:

Resolved

The motion of John E. Hall the following Resolution was adopted that the Mortgage and Lien Laws embraced in the Statutes of the Late territory of Kansas be and are hereby made the Laws of this District.

Also the folowing Resolutions which were Presented by Geo F. Griffith:

Resolved

That Resolution 1st addopted Sept 22d 1860 be so amended as to Read as folows. That all watter Lode Gulch or Patch Claims now held according to the Laws of this District shal be held without improvement until the 10th day of July AD 1861 after which time every individual or Company shal in person or by their Agent Work at Least one of his or their Claims one day in every Week. Provided Any person or Company who are actual Residents of this District and actively employed in Any business for himself or for another shal Lawfully hold all Claims that he or they may have by virtue of his or their Residence being in this District

Resolved:

That any Legal Claim Holder desiring to return to the States May by paying to the Judge of the Miners Court a fee of $1.00 and filing an affidavit with Judges Docket That it [is] Necessary for him to be absent and that in his absence that it is impossible for him to Lawfully Work his Claims Shal hold the Same without work for the Space of Eight Months.

Resolved:

That the first ten Ladies who may become Residents of this District Each be permitted to Select One Unoccupied Town Lot within the District and upon being Recorded to be held unto them as Real Estate.

On Motion
Meeting adjourned

George F. Secretary 2
Griffith 1

Declaration of the returns of an Election held in this District Saturday June 8th 1861 for the purpose of Electing a Sheriff for the Unexpired term occasioned by the Removal of J M Lain from this District. Henry Chapeze having been voted for according to the Election Laws of this District and having received the Greatest number of Votes for that office was declared duly Elected Sheriff of this District.

June 22d 1861

Miners Met Pursuant to Call of President for the purpose of Reconsidering a Resolution passed on the 8th June and any other business that might Come before the Meeting.

On Motion the folowing Resolutions were unanimously addopted

Resolved

That the Resolution passed at a meeting on the 8th inst requiring Nonresidents to work one of his or their Claims one day in every week is hereby repealed & the folowing be substituted in its place

Resolved:

That all Claims liable by previously existing Laws to forfeiture or repreemption upon the 10th day of July next May be held unimproved thereafter Provided the Claim Holder shal upon said 10th day of July by himself or agent pay to the Recorder into the Treasury of the District a yearly Tax of twenty five cents upon each & every such Claim, or Provided the Claim Holder is a resident of this District or Provided the Claim Holder shal work by himself or his agent one of his Claims within this District to the Amount of One days work to every Week Then in either case his Claims shal remain Valid but nothing herein Contained shal be so Construed as to Conflict with the Tunnel Law

Resolved:

That Sec 12th of the Laws Governing the Miners Court be & is hereby repealed and that the folowing be substituted in their place

Resolved:

That either party feeling agrieved may appeal from a decision of a Jury of three or the Judge to a Jury of Six or to a Jury of Not exceeding twelve to be decided upon by the parties Provided the party is appealing shal give notice of his intention to appeal within Twenty Four hours after the rendition of Judgement And provided he shal first pay all costs that have already accrued within five days after Judgement is rendered. Also further Resolved that when an appeal is taken as herein provided or by Law required it shal be the duty of the Jury of the Miners Court to make out a transcript of the Record in the Case Together with any special Ruling Made in the trial when either party requires it And Complies with the Law authorizing an appeal The Judges fees to be one Dollar for such transcrip

Resolved:

That Sec 2 of Chap 4th of the Revised Laws of this District Be and are Hereby so amended to Read as folows after the word District in the Sixth Line of Said Section and in immediately before the word at," Or holds property with this District."

On Motion Meeting adopted that the 1 pr of these Resolutions be Copied in the Rocky Mountain News

On Motion Meeting adjourned
Georgetown June 22d 1861
Geo F Griffith Secretary
By DTG. Deputy Recorder

July 17th 1862 [1861]

Miners met pursuant to call of president and the folowing Resolutions were unanimously addopted

Resolved 1st That all claims now held valid either by preemption, Repreemption, or purchase in this District Shal be held as Real Estate from and after this Date

2d That Section 1st of Chapter 14th of the Revised Laws of this District be so ammended as to Read as Follows The Defendent in any Cause in which suit is not already commenced shal have the right of redemption on any Real Estate or personal property to the amt. of $350.00 or over by paying to the Court for the Benefit of the Purchaser the amount of the purchase money together with interest at the rate of 20 per cent per Month if paid within 30 days from date of said sale.

3d That all Discovery Claims Lawfully Recorded since the 22d Day of September 1860 and all Discovery Claims that may be hereafter taken shal be Two Hundred feet in Length and of the Width of other Lode Claims. And all Discovery Claims now taken Claimed and Recorded shal be held free from Execution attachment or forced Sale

4th Resolved that when suit in any cause is hereafter instituted in the Miners Court of this District, such suit shal then become a Lien upon the property of the Defendent that is not exempt from Levy and Sale upon execution belonging to the defendent in this District.

On Motion Meeting adjourned
Griffith Mining District July 17th 1861

Geo. F. Griffith — Secretary
By D. T. Griffith — Deputy Recorder

Note

1. A much earlier transcription of these laws appears in Clarence King, comp., *The United States Mining Laws and Regulations thereunder, and State and Territorial Mining Laws to which are Appended Local Mining Rules and Regulations.* Tenth Census (Washington, D.C.: Department of the Interior, Census Office, 1885).

Appendix 2

The Family of Jefferson and Sidney Griffith

Records deposited in the State Historical Society of Missouri, 1020 Lowry Street, Columbia, Missouri 65201.

The 1850 census of Andrew County, Missouri showed the following information about the Griffith family:

PARENTS:

Griffith, Jefferson, born in Kentucky, age 47
Griffith, Sidney, born in Kentucky, age 47

CHILDREN OF JEFFERSON AND SIDNEY GRIFFITH:

Griffith, John S., born in Kentucky, age 19
Griffith, George F., born in Kentucky, age 17
Griffith, Sarah L., born in Kentucky, age 15
Griffith, David T., born in Kentucky, age 14 (according to the 1856 census in Liberty Township, Mills County, Iowa)
Griffith, Mary A., born in Indiana, age 13
Griffith, Daniel F., born in Indiana, age 10
Griffith, Nancy J., born in Indiana, age 6

The 1856 Iowa State Census of Liberty Township, Mills County, Iowa, revealed the following:

John S. Griffith: Listed as twenty-five years old, an attorney, who had lived in Mills County for three years. He was married to

Elvira, twenty years old, a native of Ohio who had lived in Iowa for three years. George and Elvira had a one-year-old son, George A., who was born in Iowa.

David T. Griffith: Listed as sixteen years old, a merchant, who had resided in Iowa for two years. He lived with Columbus and Leah Nuckolls's family.

Sarah Griffith Sampson: Listed as married to Ezra B. Sampson, whom she had married on September 12, 1853, in Mills County, Iowa. Sarah and Ezra Sampson had a one-year-old son named James.

Nancy J. Griffith: Accompanied her sister Sarah to Glenwood, Iowa, from Missouri and lived in the home of the Sampsons. Although the record is not clear, Sidney Griffith apparently died in Missouri, so Nancy was left in the care of her sister.

Mary Griffith: Married William Renshaw and resided in White County, Illinois (Book "K," 470, Clear Creek County Archives, Clear Creek County, Georgetown, Colorado).

Jefferson and George F. Griffith: Appeared in Cass County, Nebraska, at Plattsmouth during February, 1857 (Quitclaim deed dated February 16, 1857, Office of the Cass County Clerk, Plattsmouth, Nebraska).

William Griffith was the only Griffith connected with the Georgetown family for whom I could find no information prior to his arrival in Colorado. Whether he was a much older son and brother or perhaps a cousin who attached himself to the family in Colorado, I have not been able to uncover to date. I suspect he was a cousin. I believe this since he was not listed as an heir of Jefferson Griffith as were his known children, both in Iowa and in Colorado.

Glossary

bar: A sand deposit containing valuable ore, usually found underwater close to the bank of a stream.

bar-diggings: Accumulations of gold-bearing gravel along the banks of a stream, which miners worked when the water was low or by means of cofferdams.

bullion: Refined gold and silver that was formed into bars or ingots instead of coin.

cap or caprock: Barren rock or soil that covered an ore deposit. It also could be an ore pinch out.

chute or shute: An inclined trough above ground, through which ore fell or was "shot" by gravity from a higher to a lower level.

claim: The portion of mining ground held under federal and local laws by one claimant or association, after being located and recorded.

cofferdam: A temporary watertight enclosure from which water was pumped to expose the bottom of a body of water to permit mining.

cord: A volume measure originally used for fuel wood, a pile 8 feet long, 4 feet high, and 4 feet wide, equaling 128 cubic feet. The miners did not possess scales to weigh the ore, so this measure was used instead.

crevice: A shallow fissure in the bedrock under a gold placer, which contained small but highly concentrated deposits of gold. Also, a fissure containing a vein of mineral.

diggings: A term applicable to all mineral deposits and mining camps, but used in the United States to mean placer mining.

district: In the United States and territories west of the Missouri River, this was a vaguely bounded and temporary division and organization created by the inhabitants of a mining region. A district possessed one code of mining laws and one recorder. Counties and county officers gradually replaced these basic arrangements.

gulch claim: As used by Colorado gold rush participants, a gulch claim was a placer operation. It was located in a canyon along a stream bed where gold could be extracted by placer methods.

lode: A vein in the country-rock containing mineral. This term applied to only metalliferous leads composed of quartz or other rock *in place*, not an alluvial deposit in a stream, which would be called a placer.

outcrop: A vein that emerged at the surface of the ground (often located on a mountain side) or appeared immediately under the soil.

patch diggings: Patch claims measured fifty feet by sixty feet and were located on hillsides along old river terraces above bar and creek placer operations. The miners called them "patch" claims because their gold seemed to appear only in pockets, although they reputedly continued all the way to bedrock. Their biggest drawback was lack of water, which miners often hauled a couple of miles to work these claims.

placer: A spot where gold could be recovered from sand or gravel by washing. Legally, it included any deposit, except veins, quartz lodes, or any other rock permanently in place.

preemption: The acquisition before others of the surface of land to be used for agriculture. However, the early Colorado miners used it to denote claiming land for mining purposes.

real estate (miners' definition)**:** A piece of claimed real estate that was not forfeitable even if the owner was absent from the district.

sluicing: Washing gold-bearing dirt through long boxes with riffled bottoms called sluices. The sluices allowed the heavier ore to settle out, while the dirt was carried away in the water.

stamp mill: A machine as well as the structure housing it in which rock was crushed to a desired fineness by descending stamps (usually five to a battery), operated by water or steam power.

water claim: A claim taken for a specified amount of water removed from a stream to be used for mining, after which it would be returned to the stream. (William Greever, *The Bonanza West*, 164.)

water power: The descent of water in a stream from which power may be obtained to operate machinery. The amount of water in a stream necessary to make machinery function.

Bibliography

Newspapers

Rocky Mountain News, 13 August 1859; 10 September 1859; 27 October 1859; 8 December 1859; 11 January 1860; 18 January 1860; 6 March 1860; 21 March 1860; 16 May 1860; 22 December 1860; 6 March 1861; 10 April 1861; 12 April 1861; 27 April 1861; 2 May 1861; 4 May 1861.

Denver Bulletin, 9 May 1860.

Georgetown Courier, 4 August 1900; 10 February 1912.

(Georgetown) *Mining Review*, January 1873.

Articles

August, Ray. "Gringos vs. Mineros: The Hispanic Origins of Western American Mining Law." *Western Legal History: The Journal of the Ninth Judicial Circuit Historical Society* (summer/fall 1996).

Dubbs, Henry A. "The Unfolding of the Law in the Rocky Mountain Region." *The Colorado Magazine* 3, no. 4 (October 1926).

Fritz, Percy Stanley. "The Constitutions and Laws of Early Mining Districts—In Boulder County, Colorado." *University of Colorado Studies* 21, no. 2 (March 1934).

Frost, Aaron. "History of Clear Creek County," *History of Clear Creek and Boulder Valleys, Colorado.* Reprint. Evansville, Ind.: Unigraphic, Inc., 1971.

Marshall, Thomas Maitland. "Miners' Laws of Colorado." *American Historical Review* 25 (April 1920).

Reid, John Phillip. "Punishing the Elephant: Malfeasance and Organized Criminality on the Overland Trail." *Montana, the Magazine of Western History* 47, no. 1 (spring 1997).

Rogers, James Grafton. "The Mining District Governments of the West: Their Interest and Literature." *Law Library Journal* 28 (July 1935).

Willing, George M. "Diary of a Journey to the Pike's Peak Gold Mines in 1859." Edited by Ralph P. Bieber. *Mississippi Valley Historical Review* 14, no. 3 (December 1927).

Books

Bakken, Gordon Morris. *The Development of Law on the Rocky Mountain Frontier, Civil Law and Society, 1850–1912*. Contributions in Legal Studies, no. 27. Westport, Conn.: Greenwood Press, 1983.

Bigney, T. O., and S. S. Wallihan. *The Rocky Mountain Directory and Colorado Gazetteer for 1871. . . .* Denver: S. S. Wallihan and Company, 1870.

Cushman, Samuel. *The Mines of Clear Creek County, Colorado*. Denver: Times Steam Printing House, 1876.

Digerness, David S. *The Mineral Belt*, vol. III, *Georgetown–Mining–Colorado Central Railroad*. Silverton, Colo.: Sundance Publications, Limited, 1982.

Fossett, Frank. *Colorado: Historical, Descriptive and Statistical Work on the Rocky Mountain Gold and Silver Mining Region*. Denver: Daily Tribune Steam Printing House, 1876.

———. *Colorado: Its Gold and Silver Mines, Farms and Ranges, and Health and Pleasure Resorts*. New York: C. G. Crawford, 1880.

Fritz, Percy Stanley. *Colorado: The Centennial State*. New York: Prentice Hall, Inc., 1940.

Greever, William S. *The Bonanza West*. Norman: University of Oklahoma Press, 1963.

Hafen, LeRoy R., ed. *Colorado and Its People: A Narrative and Topical History of the Centennial State*. Vol. 1. New York: Lewis Historical Publishing Company, Inc., 1948.

Hall, Frank. *History of the State of Colorado*. Vol. 3. Chicago: Blakely Printing Company, 1889–1893.

Henderson, Charles W. *Mining in Colorado: A History of Discovery, Development and Production*. United States Geological Survey Professional Paper 138. Washington, D.C.: Government Printing Office, 1926.

Hollister, Ovando J. *The Mines of Colorado*. Springfield, Mass.: Samuel Bowles and Company, 1867.

Hughes, J. Donald. *American Indians in Colorado*. Boulder, Colo.: Pruett Publishing Company, 1977.

Mumey, Nolie, ed. *Anselm Holcomb Barker, 1822–1895, Pioneer Builder and Early Settler of Auraria; His Diary of 1858 from Plattsmouth, Nebraska Territory, to Cherry Creek Diggings, the Present Site of Denver, Colorado*. Denver: Golden Bell Press, 1959.

Richardson, Albert D. *Beyond the Mississippi: From the Great River to the Great Ocean . . . 1857–1867*. Hartford, Conn.: American Publishing Company, 1867.

Rowe, John. *The Hard Rock Men: Cornish Immigrants and the North American Frontier*. Liverpool, U.K.: Barnes and Noble, 1974.

Smith, Duane A. *Rocky Mountain Mining Camps: The Urban Frontier*. Bloomington: Indiana University Press, 1967.

Ubbelohde, Carl, Maxine Benson, and Duane A. Smith. *A Colorado History*. 7th ed. Boulder, Colo.: Pruett Publishing Company, 1995.

Public Documents and Manuscripts

Broder Bund Family Archives. CD317. Census Index. U.S. Selected Counties, 1850.

Griffith District Gold Company, "Prospectus." Western History Department, Denver Public Library, Mi-Co Mines. Griffith District, Clear Creek County, Colorado..

King, Clarence, comp. *The United States Mining Laws and Regulations thereunder, and State and Territorial Mining Laws to which are Appended Local Mining Rules and Regulations. Tenth Census*. Washington, D.C. Department of Interior, Census Office, 1885.

Griffith District Index to Book "A." Office of the Clear Creek County Archivist, Georgetown, Colorado.

Griffith Mining District, Book "A." Office of the Clear Creek County Archivist, Georgetown, Colorado.

Iowa District, Book "A." Office of the Clear Creek County Archivist, Georgetown, Colorado.

Private Acts, Session Laws of Colorado, 1861. An Act to Incorporate the Central City and Georgetown Wagon Road Company, Section 2. (Denver: Thos. Gibson, Colorado Republican Herald Office, 463–465). *Legislative Assembly of the Territory of Colorado, Begun and Held at Denver, Colorado Territory, Sept. 9th, 1861.*

Spurr, Josiah E., and George H. Garrey. *Economic Geology of the Georgetown Quadrangle (Together with the Empire District), Colorado.* United States Geological Survey Professional Paper 63. Washington, D.C.: Government Printing Office, 1908.

Willits, W. C. Map of Brown Sherman Republican and Leavenworth Mountains. Compiled from the Official Records. Denver, Colo., 1878.

———. Map of Georgetown. Denver, Colo., 1878.

"Wilson and Cass Gold Mining Company, Cash Book, 1864–1870." A photocopy of this document is in the possession of Silvia Pettem of Longmont, Colorado.

Glossary Sources

Fay, Albert H. *A Glossary of the Mining and Mineral Industry*. United States Department of the Interior, Bulletin 95. 1920; reprint Washington, D.C.: United States Government Printing Office, 1948.

Raymond, R. W. "A Glossary of Mining and Metallurgical Terms." *Transactions of the American Institute of Mining and Metallurgical Engineers*, vol. 9 (May 1880 to February 1881). Easton, Pa.: The Institute, 1881, 99–102.

Thrush, Paul W., and the staff of the Bureau of Mines, eds. and comps. *A Dictionary of Mineral and Related Terms*. Washington, D.C.: United States Department of the Interior, 1968.

Index

Page numbers in italics indicate illustrations.